The Fund-Raising Handbook

Robert L. Krit

ScottForesman
ProfessionalBooks
An Imprint of ScottForesman

To Missy, Maggie, Justin, and Kelsey

Page 2, Reprinted from "Understanding Philanthropy: Fund Raising in Perspective," by permission of the AAFRC Trust for Philanthropy. Page 19, Passages from *Bulletin on Public Relations and Development for Colleges and Universities*, March, 1975, used by permission of Charles P. Cushman, Partner, Gonser Gerber Tinker Stuhr. Pages 43–44, Used by permission of Charles W. Ebersold, Vice President, Illinois Bell Telephone. Pages 44–46, Excerpts from speech "Profile of a Fund Raiser" used by permission of Edward C. Logelin. Pages 60–61 and 66–68, Used by permission of Robert Wiegand, The Grace Bersted Foundation. Pages 90, 93, Used by permission of William N. Clark, Retired Executive Director, The Robert R. McCormick Charitable Trust and Affiliated Trusts. Pages 91–92, Reprinted with permission from *The Foundation Directory*, 11th Edition, The Foundation Center, New York, NY, 1987. Pages 93–94, Passages from *Bulletin on Public Relations and Development for Colleges and Universities*, May, 1978, pages 1–3, used by permission of Charles P. Cushman, Partner, Gonser Gerber Tinker Stuhr. Page 94, Excerpts from a speech before the Foundation Relations Workshop of the American College Public Relations Association, November, 1962, used by permission of Dr. Manning M. Patillo. Pages 112–113 and 124–126, Reprinted from the Crusade Outline Series, by permission of the American Cancer Society, Inc. Pages 161–163, Reprinted by permission of Irving I. Rimer, Public Relations Consultant, and former Vice President for Public Relations of the American Cancer Society.

Library of Congress Cataloging-in-Publication Data

Krit, Robert L.
    The fund-raising handbook / Robert L. Krit
      p.   cm.
    Includes index.
    ISBN 0-673-46242-0
    1. Fund raising—Handbooks, manuals, etc.   I. Title.
HG177.K75   1991   90-8667
658.15′224—dc20   CIP

ISBN 0-673-46242-0

PREFACE

*T*his book was written for use by everyone who is directly or indirectly involved in fund development. Included in this category are professionals, chief executive officers, academic officials, members of governing boards, corporate and private foundation officials, trust officers, other estate planners, clergy, and all of the men and women who make up America's distinguished volunteer force.

The book is intended to serve as a resource of comprehensive guidelines for the planning, preparation, and implementation of fund-raising operations of any size—from small organizations that are just beginning their fund development programs to large and well-established ones.

Its contents are constructed around the basic principles of development that I have learned, observed, and applied during almost forty years of experience as a chief development officer, campaign director, board member, and volunteer.

Every part of this book is geared, in one way or another, to help you achieve success in your fund-raising program by incorporating the following traditional elements into your operation:

- Sound management
- A well-constructed case
- Good planning
- Thorough preparation
- Careful selection, training, and utilization of volunteers
- Adherence to a realistic timetable

- An eye on the budget
- A healthy and continual infusion of human dynamics

Because of the importance of these elements, I have made repeated references to them—in some considerable detail—throughout the book.

CONTENTS

ACKNOWLEDGMENTS

I would like to express my appreciation to the many distinguished volunteer leaders and staff executives who have played major roles in my own career development. I regret that space limitations make it impossible for me to list all of them, but two people have especially enriched my understanding and perception of how effective fund-raising works. The first is Herman M. Finch, chairman of the Board of Trustees of the University of Health Sciences/The Chicago Medical School, whose total dedication, faith, and strong leadership inspired those around him to respond generously to the needs of that institution. Generating a spirit of family pride and tradition, in the face of numerous obstacles, Mr. Finch was chiefly responsible for the university's growth to a level that few thought possible. The second person is the late Harold J. (Sy) Seymour, who is regarded by most of us in the field as the architect of classic fund development as it is practiced today. I had the privilege of serving with Mr. Seymour for a three-year period on the American Cancer Society's national Campaign Advisory Committee, and I benefited greatly from his wise counsel.

I also would like to thank the following individuals and organizations, who contributed to this book in a more direct manner:

> *Irving I. Rimer*, consultant and former Vice-President for Public Relations for the American Cancer Society, Inc., for his excellent capsule of "6 Basic Steps to Follow in Setting Up a Public Relations Program."

William N. Clark, former executive director of the Robert R. McCormick Charitable Trust, former Chairman of the Board of The Donors' Forum of Chicago, and former Financial Editor of The Chicago Tribune, for his valuable input in the chapter on foundation relations.

Dr. Manning M. Patillo, President Emeritus of Oglethorpe University, former President of The Foundation Center, and former Associate Director of The Danforth Foundation, for permission to use excerpts from his 1962 speech at The Foundation Relations Workshop of the American College Public Relations Association.*

Mrs. Marion Faldet, Vice President and Secretary, The Spencer Foundation, and Gonser Gerber Tinker Stuhr, for permission to use excerpts from her speech, "Foundation Turn-offs and Turn-ons," made in 1978 at a foundation workshop of G.G.T. and S.*

Maurice G. Gurin, Chairman of the American Association of Fund-Raising Counsel Trust for Philanthropy, and Professor *Jon VanTil*, of Rutgers University, for permission to use their article, "Understanding Philanthropy: Fund-Raising in Perspective."

National Headquarters, *American Cancer Society, Inc.*, for permission to use selections from its Campaign Guidebooks.

J. Jay Gerber, former Vice President for Development, Northwestern University, and senior partner, Gonser Gerber Tinker Stuhr, for his recommendations on the different ways in which case statements can be used.

Charles W. Ebersold, former Vice President for Marketing, Illinois Bell Telephone Company, and former State Campaign Chairman, American Cancer Society, Illinois Division, Inc., for permission to use selections from his speech, "What a Volunteer Expects from Staff," made

---

*I have purposely chosen to include the speeches of Dr. Patillo and Mrs. Faldet to illustrate how little the basic principles of organized fund-raising have changed over the years. In recent conversations, they both confirmed this position.

at a staff conference of the American Cancer Society, Illinois Division.

The Foundation Directory, 11th edition, The Foundation Center, New York, New York, 1987, for permission to reprint selections from "Types of Foundations," "Establishment of Private Foundations," and "General Characteristics of Four Types of Foundations."

Robert A. Wiegand, attorney, former vice president, trust department, The Continental Bank, and former Director of Planned Giving at Lake Forest College, for his contributions to the chapter on planned giving.

Edward C. Logelin (an old friend, and a distinguished volunteer leader), Vice President–Midwest, United States Steel Corporation, and Gonser Gerber Tinker Stuhr, for permission to use excerpts from his speech at a 1974 development workshop.

My brother, *Norman Krit*, Manager of Financial Development, Executive Service Corps of Chicago, for his continual encouragement and many valuable suggestions during the planning stages of this book.

Amy Davis, Professional Books Group, Scott, Foresman and Company, for her invaluable counsel and support.

Lynne M. Kuderko for her assistance in the preparation and editing of the manuscript.

Finally, I want to acknowledge, with grateful appreciation, all of the talented professionals and volunteers who helped to establish and develop basic policies, procedures, and techniques that have provided sound and reliable guidelines for all nonprofit organizations that need funding from the private sector. Hopefully, this book represents their best work.

DEFINITIONS OF TERMS

Organization—Agency, institution, college, university, association, coalition, etc.

Fund-raising—Campaign, development, drive, crusade, appeal, march, income development, etc.

Case Statement—Statement of the case, statement of objectives, etc. (Extended statement of objectives that also sets forth the reasons why the organization feels that it should be supported.)

Governing Board—Board of directors, board of regents, board of managers, board of governors, board of trustees, etc.

Foundation—Trust, fund, memorial, etc.

Contribution—Gift, grant, support.

Planned Gift—Deferred gift, endowment, legacy, bequest, etc.

INTRODUCTION

*T*here is no mystique about fund-raising. Answers to fund-raising problems are never found in the seemingly endless array of gimmicks, promotions, devices, and mass-marketing programs that are so prevalent in our society. Instead, those who work in nonprofit settings should look to the basic policies, procedures, and techniques, which have been reliably tested and have not changed in the past fifty years or more. It must also be remembered that allocating funds is the principal occupation of corporation and foundation grantmakers, who are just as concerned with identifying appropriate recipients for their grants as nonprofit organizations are about having their needs met. Finally, there is no substitution for a well-documented case, presented by an enthusiastic, well-informed volunteer, representing an organization that is doing good work, to a well-researched prospect—and that is the central theme of this book.

The book is divided into five sections designed to take an organization through a complete fund-raising operation, from the initial planning and preparation stages through the campaign itself and finally through the all-important elements of cleanup, acknowledgment, and evaluation.

SECTION I

Background
and
History
of
Fund-Raising

THE BACKGROUND OF PHILANTHROPY AND FUND-RAISING

*O*ne of the most difficult parts of writing this book was to decide on an appropriate beginning. During the course of reading everything I could find that might provide the inspiration and wisdom that I was seeking, I came across a superb article written by Maurice G. Gurin, chairman of the American Association of Fund-Raising Council (AAFRC) Trust for Philanthropy and Rutgers Professor Jon Van Til, entitled, "Understanding Philanthropy: Fund-Raising in Perspective." Reading the article not only enriched my own understanding of philanthropy but also gave me a better understanding of how and where fund-raising fit into the entire picture. This article provides a valuable base of knowledge for all of us who are part of the fund-raising profession. Accordingly, this chapter features selected highlights and data taken from this article, with the kind permission of the AAFRC Trust for Philanthropy.

I was especially interested in Gurin and Van Til's definitions of philanthropy and charity, and the distinction between these two terms. The word *philanthropy* originally came from the Greek and meant "love of mankind." A more recent, popularly quoted definition was advanced by Robert L. Payton, who extended philanthropy to include voluntary giving, voluntary service, and voluntary association, primarily for the benefit of others. *Charity* is defined by Paul N. Ylvisaker as the religious tradition of altruism, compassion, and empathy, and giving on a one-to-one basis.

Today, most of us use the word *charity* in reference to helping the poor and the needy. While some voluntary organizations still provide such services, the government—at all levels—has assumed major responsibility for these unfortu-nate folks, directly and indirectly. On the other hand, philan-thropy takes a more impersonal and dispassionate approach to bettering the human condition by institutionalized giving, rec-ognizing a responsibility to the public interest, and helping to bring about necessary changes in our society.

Philanthropy, as we know it today, is concerned gener-ally with improving the quality of life for everyone by promot-ing welfare, happiness, and culture. Its general missions are found in protection of the environment, prevention of disease, improvement of education, enhancement of the arts, and pres-ervation of historic landmarks. Philanthropy also is viewed as a tradition and sector of our society—alternately referred to as the third sector, the independent sector, the voluntary sector, and the nonprofit sector. (The other three sectors are business [or for-profit], government, and household [or informal].)

How old is philanthropy? Egypt's *Book of the Dead* pro-vides a good starting point—about 4000 B.C. The Hebrews' history of religiously motivated charity goes back at least as far as the Egyptians. According to the Old Testament, Jacob prom-ised to give away a tenth of all that God gave him, and, to the best of our knowledge, that's how the practice of tithing began. Religious doctrines of every faith set high ethics for givers; the size of the gift is not considered as important as the spirit in which it is given, and the value of the gift is determined by the extent of the giver's sacrifice.

Over the years, I have heard many versions of the French social philosopher Alexis de Tocqueville's travels throughout the United States in 1831, after which he wrote: "When Amer-icans see a need in the community, the members organize into a group to meet it." He was referring, of course, to a voluntary organization. When we think of philanthropic organizations, we think generally of those organizations to which contribu-tions are tax-deductible, including churches and synagogues, as well as social service, health, education, culture, and any other category of organization that enjoys tax-exempt status.

The number of these tax-exempt organizations is stagger-ing. According to Internal Revenue Service figures, in 1987 there were 850,000, not including many religious organizations that have automatic tax exemption and many small organizations which do not need to file. Here is another figure that reflects the generosity of the American people: *Voluntary contributions in 1988 to gift-supported organizations, institutions, and agencies, exceeded $100 billion,* according to estimates in GIVING USA, the annual report of the AAFRC Trust for Philanthropy, which updates these estimates every spring. Still another statistic that should give one a feeling of pride in the American tradition was reported in a Gallup poll conducted for Independent Sector in 1988, which estimates that a total of 80 million American adults contribute some portion of their time as volunteers in behalf of philanthropic causes.

This section on the definition, history, and characteristics of philanthropy and charity provides a solid base of understanding and brings fund-raising into better focus as the means rather than the end.

HISTORY OF FUND-RAISING

The history of fund-raising is distinctly American and has developed more or less from collections of one type or another to organized campaigns requiring skilled management at both volunteer and staff levels.

The first systematic effort of any kind to raise money in America was for Harvard College. As the story goes, the Massachusetts Bay Colony, in 1641, sent three clergymen to England to solicit money for the purpose of enabling Harvard to "educate the heathen Indian" (among other objectives). Reportedly, one of the three returned with 500 pounds, one became a rector in England, and one wound up on the scaffold. After this somewhat inauspicious beginning for our noble profession, fund-raising procedures improved when Harvard, as well as Yale and William and Mary colleges, received grants from their provincial governments and from the King. Occasionally, bequests provided some additional funds. Harvard tried some lotteries, but they were unsuccessful, bringing in little money and tarnishing its good name with squabbles and law suits.

The next significant achievement of record began in 1739, when a young English evangelist, George Whitefield, started "the most famous preaching tour in American history, assailing sin and crying out against the misery of the poor." In his seven visits to the colonies, Whitefield took up collections for poor debtors, raised money for the victims of disaster, and secured books and financial assistance for (then) hard-pressed colleges, including Harvard, Dartmouth, Princeton, and the University of Pennsylvania.

During those early years, one of our leading fund-raisers was Benjamin Franklin, who apparently took time out from his better known pursuits to undertake a number of campaigns. He shrewdly planned his appeals, and had the following counsel for those who sought his advice:

> In the first place, I advise you to apply to all those whom you know will give something; next, to those whom you are uncertain whether they will give anything or not, and show them the list of those who have given; and lastly, do not neglect those whom you are sure will give nothing, for in some of them you may be mistaken.

In the nineteenth century fund-raising consisted mainly of personal solicitation, often by paid solicitors, of passing the church plate and staging church suppers and bazaars, and of writing "begging letters." Educational fund-raising was a personal search for gifts by "financial agents" who frequently were the presidents of the colleges involved. It appears that a great deal of this kind of fund-raising was carried over into the twentieth century, and seems headed for the twenty-first.

The classic campaign as we know it today began when two YMCA secretaries, Charles Sumner Ward and Lyman L. Pierce, using tightly organized methods, raised $60 million in capital funds between 1905 and 1906. In the early 1900s, Andrew Carnegie and John D. Rockefeller led the way for the advent of large-scale philanthropy and the establishment of benevolent foundations.

THE NATURE OF GIVING—AND ASKING

*. . . apply to all those whom you know will give something;
next, to those whom you are uncertain whether they will give
anything or not, and show them the list of those who have
given; and lastly, do not neglect those whom you are sure will
give nothing, for in some of them you may be mistaken.*

Benjamin Franklin

*T*here are many theories about why people give. My own
feeling is that most people want to give something back to
society out of a sense of altruism, compassion, or empathy, or
as an expression of their religious faith. Others give because
they believe in or are involved in a particular organization or
cause. Still others give because people around them are giving.
Finally, there are those who give out of respect for (or some
business or personal relationship with) the person who does
the asking.

Whatever reason lies behind a particular individual's contribution, it is important to remember that, basically, people
give to *people* and not to causes. People are more likely to give
to people who are enthusiastic, well informed, at least equal in
stature, and who themselves have made thoughtful contributions to the cause for which they seek support. With all of this
in mind, let's assume that you are the asker. *Consider this checklist of positives:*

1. Are you bold and enthusiastic in your approach?

2. Are you well informed about your organization, its history, traditions, and programs, as well as the compelling points of your appeal?
3. Have you tried to secure pertinent background information about your prospect, i.e., past giving record, position in the community, and indicated interest in the programs of your organization, as published in foundation and corporate directories?
4. Do you make appointments to see your prospects personally?
5. Are you at least equal in stature to your prospects?
6. Do you try to sell the program rather than the price tag? Do you ask the prospect to join you in doing something meaningful for the cause which you represent instead of for your dollar goal?
7. Have you made your own thoughtful gift first, so that you can have an effective reply in the event that the prospect asks how much you have given?
8. Have you made an effort to ascertain the amount that you feel the prospect should be capable of giving?
9. Do you understand the dynamics that worked in your own decision to participate and support? Can you apply any of these in your approach?

Now consider a checklist of negatives. Does your appeal include any of these?

1. "Any amount will help, no matter how small." This cheapens the campaign and defeats the premise of thoughtful, proportionate giving.
2. "This is an emergency campaign. If we don't raise (x dollars) by (a certain date) programs will be reduced or eliminated." Most people are not likely to want to get on a losing bandwagon. There are exceptions to this, however, especially in religious fund-raising.
3. "A gift of (x dollars) actually will cost you only (x dollars)." The prospect knows this (or can secure this information from other sources) and may resent your implication that the major reason for giving is the tax benefit gained.

Note: Comprehensive information about the do's and don'ts of solicitation and related matters is contained in The Volunteer Handbook that appears in a later chapter.

Additional thoughts about the nature of giving and asking:

- Too often, a request for a contribution is made apologetically. The response to this type of approach generally invokes a rejection or a token gift. Many thoughtful contributions are secured when prospects are asked to consider their support as investments in whatever the objectives of the organization happen to be, e.g., "control of cancer," "a more stable neighborhood," "reduction in drug abuse," or "quality education." Invite the individual to join you in the achievement of these objectives. Pride of association can be a strong motivating factor.
- Many successful volunteers like to begin their solicitations by telling their prospects why they themselves became involved.
- Prospects often want to know how much is being given by those closest to the asking organization, e.g., board members, alumni, campaign leaders, etc. Campaign workers should have this information readily available.

A final point to consider is that you often find your best prospects among those who have given before, and you should carefully cultivate these people for future contacts. Some organizations make the mistake of contacting past donors only when they are requesting another gift. It is important to keep donors informed of your programs and relevant events *throughout the year*, through newsletters, annual reports, and other publications reporting items of interest. By doing this, you are reporting to donors the significance of their contributions with the unstated implication, of course, of the need for continued support.

One of America's greatest philanthropists, when asked what motivated him to make a grant, replied simply, "If you can move me with your appeal, I will support you. The challenge is yours." Another philanthropist, John D. Rockefeller, Jr., saw giving in this light:

> "Some people have a less keen sense of their duty and responsibility than others. With them a little urging may be helpful. But with most people a convincing presentation of the facts and the need is far more effective. When a solicitor comes to you and lays on your heart the responsibility that rests so heavily on his; when his earnestness gives convincing evidence of how seriously interested he is; when he makes it clear that he knows you are no less anxious to do your duty in the matter than he is, that you are just as conscientious, that he feels sure all you need is to realize the importance of the enterprise and the urgency of the need in order to lead you to do your full share in meeting it—he has made you a friend and has brought you to think of giving not as a duty but as a privilege."

You are at least as good a judge of the nature of giving and asking as anyone because so much of this is subjective and personal.

SECTION II

Preparing for the Campaign

DETERMINING YOUR READINESS

A logical way to begin preparing for your campaign is to determine first your stage of readiness. Here are eight points to consider:

1. Is there wholehearted agreement among your board members concerning the worthwhileness of your cause?
2. Is your organization well regarded in the community; are your services considered important and relevant?
3. Is there a valid need for funds and can the case for supporting your organization be communicated easily and effectively?
4. Is good, influential leadership available?
5. Can enough enthusiastic volunteers be recruited to contact prospects personally?
6. Is the planning (and timing) of your campaign well-constructed and sound?
7. If you are contemplating a capital campaign, are operating funds for the facility available after it has been constructed?
8. Is the campaign adequately budgeted?

PRECAMPAIGN ACTIVITIES

*T*he crucially important job of planning and implementing all of the necessary precampaign activities provides the solid base that is integral to the success of any fund-raising operation, large or small. Ideally, planning should be started at least a year in advance of the start of the campaign to allow ample time for the recruitment, organization, and training of the necessary volunteer force, to get all of the support systems in place, and to help develop a favorable campaign climate.

Ten precampaign activities are considered to be standard in most fund-raising circles. Consider which apply to your situation.

1. Establishment of a campaign headquarters, with space for volunteers to meet, make phone calls, and generally use as their base. This should be where records are kept and where gifts are received, processed, acknowledged, and reported. This is also the place where mail is received and promptly answered.

2. Appointment of a board, committee, or council on fund development (sometimes referred to as a fund-raising committee, campaign committee, income development committee, etc.). This should be a permanent, standing committee of the board, and should be given (at least) the following responsibilities:

   A. Establishment of a plan for a long-range, comprehensive development program consisting of three major elements: the annual fund, capital and other special needs, and planned giving.

      B. Setting of immediate and long-range goals.

      C. Setting of a budget to cover costs of items such as:
- Salaries for professional and clerical support staff
- Meetings: kickoffs, report meetings, training sessions, other
- Luncheons and dinners
- Travel and transportation
- Printing
- Office supplies
- Mailings
- Public relations
- Purchase or rental of furniture, fixtures, office equipment, etc.
- Telephone
- Insurance
- Miscellaneous expenses

      D. Recruiting general campaign chairperson

      E. Assisting that individual whenever and however necessary.

      F. Reviewing, evaluation, and supporting all campaign activities and programs, including postcampaign evaluation and presenting all of the above to the full board, for its input, and approval.

      G. Helping to establish desirable giving patterns by making thoughtful, pace-setting contributions and encouraging other board members to do the same.

3. Preparation of the case statement, which is discussed later in this section.

4. Formation of a campaign plan to be presented for the input and approval of the board.

5. Determination of an operational timetable for regular and special campaign activities and events.

6. Setting up and launching a public relations program to help develop and maintain a favorable climate for the campaign.

7. Preparation of necessary campaign publications and materials, such as campaign brochures; planned giving pamphlets; handbooks for volunteers; and standard forms for reporting, recording, and acknowledging gifts and pledges, volunteer recruitment, prospect assignments, and so on.

8. Completion of prospect research:
   A. To provide information about the interests and resources of your present major prospects, and any special connection that they may have with your organization, such as past donors, alumni or alumni within family units, recipients of assistance or service, participants or supporters of programs similar to yours, and individuals who have been cured or known to have lost loved ones to a particular disease or other health-related problem within the scope of your organization's programs.
   B. To recommend new prospects both for major gifts and for general solicitation.
9. Procurement of pace-setting advance gifts to help establish a desirable giving pattern.
10. Establishment of an efficient system of records, reports, and other good accounting procedures.

What You Can Do Tomorrow: The Campaign Plan

1. Go through a checklist of campaign plan components and prepare a draft, using the sample plan as a guide unless you have one of your own that is more suitable for your situation. Incorporate recommendations from the committee that evaluated your last campaign.
2. List all of the campaign budget items you can think of, including those that were contained in the budget for the previous year.
3. In consultation with your controller or your accountant, make necessary estimates of cost increases—if any—of the basic budget items.
4. In consultation with other members of your staff, estimate areas of increased cost due to such things as an anticipated expansion of the campaign organization requiring additional staff, additional travel, additional meetings, and additional materials. *Note:* In some instances, the estimated costs for your upcoming campaign might be lower than those of the previous year because of a change in strategy, such as shifting from mailings to personal solicitation.

5. Assemble all of your deliberations, together with a draft of your campaign plan for presentation to, and discussion with, one or more of the following individuals:
   - Your chief executive officer,
   - Your board committee or development person,
   - Your governing board chairperson, and
   - The general campaign chairperson.

DEVELOPING THE CASE STATEMENT

Most of us have heard about case statements, and opinions vary about how one should be constructed and what it should contain. There is no single formula, but most good case statements follow fairly similar patterns.

A case statement has been described as the rationale for the very existence of an organization, as well as for its growth and development. It is also a selling document, its purpose being to obtain acceptance and support from the key people within the organization's constituencies. Where appropriate, it should show how society as a whole will benefit from the success of the campaign.

Ideally, the person who is closest to the organization and who knows the most about it writes the first draft. Case statements go through several drafts, securing the input of all levels of leadership and eventually putting everyone—staff and volunteers alike—on the same wavelength, pointed at the same goals, and speaking the same language.

The six basic elements of a case statement are as follows:

1. *Description of the organization.*
   - Why was the organization founded?
   - What role does it play in its professional community?
   - If it were not in existence today, would there be a justification or a need to found it?
   - What is distinctive about it?
   - Why should it be preserved and strengthened?

2. *Description of the organization's service, programs, and growth.*
   - Whom does the organization serve?
   - How does it serve?
   - How has it grown, not only in size, but also in meeting the needs for which it was founded, or the needs which have since developed and have become part of its mission?
   - What are the measurable results of its programs and services?

3. *Long-range plans—new directions.*
   - What are the organization's long-range plans?
   - What are its new directions?

4. *New or additional resources that will be required to fund those objectives.*
   - New construction, renovations, remodeling, new equipment
   - Expanded operational needs

5. *The campaign plan.*
   - The specific goals, length of duration, organization, campaign leadership, sources of campaign work force, timetable, sources of support, range of gifts needed, commemorative gift opportunities, ways in which support can be given (cash, pledges, securities, real property, deferred gifts), etc.

6. *Volunteer leadership and sponsorship.*
   - Who comprises the volunteer leadership in the organization, e.g., the board of directors, and any sponsoring or advisory groups such as women's boards, citizen boards, or visiting committees, churches, alumni organizations.

Referring to case statements, Harold J. (Sy) Seymour said, "The case for support should aim high, provide perspective, arouse a sense of history and continuity, convey a feeling of importance, relevance and urgency and have whatever stuff it needs to warm the heart and stir the mind."

A long-time friend, Jay Gerber, former vice president for development at Northwestern University and founding partner, Gonser, Gerber, Tinker & Stuhr recommend the following five ways in which case statements can be used effectively:

1. *Securing Consensus.* The case statement is valuable in obtaining consensus about the organization's priorities, the directions envisioned, the resources deemed most crucial, the avenues of services to be stressed and opened up, and the organization's thrust in its markets. In the early stages, the case statement might go through many drafts, which representatives of key groups within the organization read and revise. Through this process, a general agreement develops concerning priorities, aims, and financial goals.
2. *Recruiting Volunteer Leadership.* The case statement is useful in recruiting key leaders for a major development effort. This must be done early in the planning phase, even before any brochures are printed. The case statement, which shows specific reasons for the extent of and goals of the campaign, helps answer questions of prospective campaign leaders and workers and gives them confidence in the planning and direction.
3. *Obtaining Major Gifts.* Often in a major development effort a proposal for a major prospect is required. Even in draft form, a case statement with a personalized cover and a personalized approach keyed to a particular donor can be an effective tool in solicitation.
4. *Testing the Market.* The case statement can be used to determine how the potential major donor feels about the proposed campaign. It brings the prospective major donor into the planning process and allows the donor to react to the proposed objectives.
5. *Forming a Basis for the "Sales" Brochure.* Finally, the case statement, once consensus has been reached by the powers that be, is the basis for campaign materials.

What You Can Do Tomorrow: Statement of the Case

1. Ask your general campaign chairman or the chairperson of your governing board (if your campaign chairperson has not yet been recruited) to call a meeting of a special committee to plan the construction of this important document. Those invited should include the chairperson of the governing board's development committee (if there is one in place), the chief executive officer, the staff campaign director, and any other individual whose input is considered to be valuable.
2. Begin to assemble some of the raw data and the specific items of information that your chairperson might wish to consider for inclusion in a rough draft for circulation (of copies) among the committee members prior to the meeting.

RECORDS AND REPORTS

*A*n efficient system of record keeping and reporting is absolutely essential to the success of any fund-raising operation. In such a system, there is a two-way flow of information, into the organization headquarters and out to the donors and the campaign volunteers.

Good records do a number of important things:

- They make it possible to measure the progress and effectiveness of volunteers.
- They make it possible to provide key and timely information to campaign leaders so that they can function effectively within their respective areas of responsibility.
- They make it possible to assure donors of restricted gifts that their wishes are being carried out.
- They make it possible to give proper credit to donors, volunteers, and others who play supporting roles in the campaign, such as media executives and public officials.
- They provide a basis for planning each year's campaign.
- They identify prospects for solicitation.
- They provide complete and accurate information about prospects to staff and volunteer workers.
- They make available a barometer of the campaign potential.
- They indicate which phases of the campaign require special attention and strengthening.
- They avoid duplicate solicitation of prospects.

The exact design of record and reporting systems vary, of course, with the structure and needs of different organizations. However, in addition to the standard criteria that are required for auditing purposes, there are basic principles that should be considered for any operation involving the handling of other people's money.

First, before designing a record system for your organization, determine the job for which each record is to be used. To assist you in doing this, consider the following factors:

- What information is needed to accomplish your purpose?
- Is the information really vital?
- How is it to be used?
- Who uses it and in what manner?
- Is it easily understandable and answerable?

Second, every record system should include these three major categories of basic information:

1. *About Volunteers.* Names, addresses, phone numbers, campaign assignments, quality of performance, dates enrolled, names of recruiters, known reasons for interest, giving record, other affiliations, memberships, honors, awards, etc.
2. *About Donors.* All of the above, except the names of the *solicitors* instead of the *recruiters*, and the following data: amounts of gifts, dates of gifts, restrictions, pledge payment schedules (if applicable), and any additional relevant information.
3. *About Prospects.* Names, addresses, phone numbers, business and other affiliations, sources of identification, gifts made to other organizations, and any additional relevant information.

In cases of corporations, foundations, and clubs and organizations, the same general information as that indicated above should be recorded with the appropriate addition (or substitution) of the names of the chief executive officers and/or the individuals who are designated as the key contacts.

Records and reports systems vary widely from one organization to another. However, the following seven principles should be regarded as basic guidelines for all to consider:

1. All records should be maintained in one central office.
2. A policy should be established specifying the office responsible for maintaining a record of all gifts received, with special attention given to designating restrictions in all appropriate records and reports.
3. All gifts should be directed to this office for recording and processing.
4. A policy should be set for consideration of specific gift restrictions. Some donors' restrictions may be unacceptable because they commit the institution to undesirable obligations.
5. Gifts should be posted and acknowledged daily.
6. The system should accommodate large gifts on the same basis as small ones.
7. No acknowledgment should be sent out containing typographical errors, erasures, or corrections.

Finally, a sound record system should be simple and flexible, so that it can be adjusted or amended to meet whatever changing needs the organization may face in the future.

OPERATIONAL TIMETABLE

A comprehensive, realistic timetable plays an indispensable role in the efficient operation of any campaign, irrespective of its size or nature.

This acts as a control mechanism to ensure that each element and phase of the campaign is completed in proper sequence—from the earliest planning stage through the following phases:

- Organization
- Advance (major) gifts
- Cultivation
- Campaign
- Evaluation

The timetable then continues through all of the traditional elements of the campaign, beginning with the writing, processing, and eventual approval of the case statement, from the first draft to the finished product, and then, in sequence:

- Recruitment and orientation of volunteers at all levels of the campaign organization.
- Identification, rating, and assignment of prospects.
- Preparation of necessary publications and other campaign materials.
- Advance major gifts and regular solicitation, in sequence.
- Kickoff and report meetings.
- Special events
- Clean-up

- Acknowledgments
- Evaluation

Your timetable should be carefully constructed with input from campaign leaders to ensure that key dates are compatible with their business and social schedules, and to help ensure that your important activities and events do not conflict with holidays or other major events in your community.

You should allow ample time in your timetable for the efficient accomplishment of each campaign task, and you should maintain ongoing vigilance to see that all deadlines are being met. Every member of the campaign task force must clearly understand that the operational timetable must be followed to the letter. It must be understood also that failure to do this can result in a breakdown of the entire campaign.

Finally, the timetable must be flexible so that changes and adjustments can be made when and where necessary. *Note:* Timetables necessarily differ greatly from one another, both in format and content. Yours must be tailored to fit the component parts of your campaign operation.

STANDARDS OF GIVING

*I*n most major campaigns and in virtually all capital campaigns, it is essential that giving standards be established at a proportionately high enough level so that a minimum of 85 percent of goal from 15 percent of donors can be achieved. Accordingly, every major gift prospect must be carefully rated to determine the level of the gift that should be requested. The rating should be based on the estimated ability of the prospect to contribute in relationship to the campaign goal.

It is extremely helpful—some say necessary—to set up a gift table as a guideline to project the sizes and numbers of gifts necessary to reach the goal. Following is a sample gift table that was used in a capital campaign conducted some years ago by a large eastern university:

Goal: $51,300,000	Needed		Received	
Size of Gift	*Approx. no. donors*	*Approx. amount*	*no. donors*	*Amount*
$1,000,000 and over	10	$15,000,000	9	$16,165,396
100,000 and over	100	18,000,000	107	24,543,879
10,000 and over	500	10,000,000	499	10,723,475
1,000 and over	3,000	7,000,000	3,208	6,887,380
Under 1,000	17,000	3,000,000	14,102	2,391,237
Total	20,610	$53,000,000	17,925	$60,711,367

You should construct a gift table to fit the nature of your campaign and the size of your goal during the goal-setting process.

PROSPECT IDENTIFICATION AND RESEARCH

*P*rospect research is discussed in great length in a number of other places in this book. But because it is as an essential first step in obtaining sufficient numbers of contributions of a thoughtful, proportionate nature, you must carefully determine the number and size of the gifts that you will need in order to reach your goal, and who will give them.

A good source of prospects are former donors, foundations, and corporations whose interests match yours, and certain members of the organizational family such as board members, members of advisory committees, and local independent businesses. Do not overload your prospect list with names from membership directories of country and other private clubs simply because they represent affluence. Concentrate instead on those individuals who have a known interest in or relationship to your organization. Then rate all of your major prospects to determine in what level of giving they should be categorized.

Prospect research should be designed to identify everything about the prospect that the worker should know:

- Past records of giving and voluntary services to your, or another, organization.
- Business affiliation and the company's record of participation in community affairs.

Be sure to give your governing board members and other volunteers an opportunity to recommend certain individuals or companies for inclusions on your prospect lists.

Do not clutter your prospect lists with names that do not have any discernable interest in your organization or its programs. Instead, identify your markets and then carefully research and analyze all of your prospect sources, choosing only those which have a rationale for their selection.

What You Can Do Tomorrow: Prospect Research

1. Determine whether your prospect list contains all of your logical markets. For example, does your list include all of the independent neighborhood businesses?
2. Begin to assemble background information about your major prospects, including past giving records and other information.
3. Ask your campaign chairperson to consider the organization of a special task force to rate prospects, and to form a plan for increasing the number of major prospects if needed.

THE NATURE OF THE VOLUNTEER

It is one of the most beautiful compensations of life that no man can sincerely try to help another without helping himself.
Ralph Waldo Emerson

*E*very nonprofit organization which uses volunteers should have a plan for bringing the volunteers into the organization, using them efficiently, and retaining their interest and their involvement.

In order to recruit and use volunteers successfully, you should know something about why they volunteer:

1. They recognize the need for united action to meet a common problem.
2. They need to belong, to serve, to join in group action.
3. They have suffered because of a particular problem and want to help "fight the disease" or "improve the condition."
4. They are searching for knowledge about a particular program or problem.
5. They want recognition of their service to the community.
6. They feel contacts made in volunteer service can be of value in business and in the improvement of their social life.
7. They need to feel worthwhile. One psychiatrist found that volunteering helped ease depression.
8. They want to give service in return for service that they received from the agency.
9. They have a desire to keep active.

Understanding of the motivations of particular volunteers makes it possible to arrange assignments that match their underlying desires.

Because many campaign volunteers are drawn from the year-round volunteer (program) force, organizations should consider some rules (criteria) for the acceptance of candidates for volunteer service. Here are some suggestions:

1. Understand the volunteer's abilities or capacities to learn and adapt, as assessed by the director of volunteers (if you have one) and/or the appropriate staff professionals.
2. Determine whether the volunteer is willing to learn and understands the need for orientation and the need to carry out the directions of the professional staff or the chairman of a particular volunteer unit.
3. Make sure the volunteer can provide regular periods of service and be a team worker.

An organization should not accept a prospective volunteer unless it can provide assignments that fit that person's capabilities.

A dean at an eastern university, in a speech to a national conference on social welfare, cautioned nonprofit organizations against making commitments to recruit volunteers (not just campaign volunteers) unless or until that organization is able to answer the following twelve questions to its own satisfaction:

1. Is there a readily observable need for volunteer services, and can this be translated into clearly defined jobs for volunteers?
2. Are we clear enough as to our professional tasks so that we may understand our own roles in relation to the volunteers?
3. Can we budget the staff time needed for effective implementation of volunteer programs?
4. Have paid staff members, at all levels, been involved in thinking through the proposal to use volunteers in agency programs, and will they give support to the activities?
5. What are our expectations of the level of volunteer performance? Are we prepared for unevenness of service and turnover of workers that is almost always a part of such programs?

6. Will we be able to assign one central staff person to supervise volunteer activities?
7. Are we willing to supervise and train new recruits?
8. Are we ready to accept the volunteers as colleagues, and to give them appropriate recognition for their services?
9. Will we welcome volunteers from all social classes in the community so that our volunteer group will be truly representative of the community that supports us?
10. Are we ready to use volunteer participation at every appropriate level of agency service, up to and including policy making?
11. Are we prepared to modify agency programs in the light of volunteer contributions and possible enrichment of programs?
12. Will we help the volunteer see the program's implications for the whole community? Will we be comfortable with and able to encourage the social action of volunteers, which should come from enlightened participation?

THE VOLUNTEER'S RIGHTS

In the words of a nationally renowned authority on volunteerism, "The voice of the volunteer has hardly been heard above an occasional whisper." In some excerpts from a thoughtful, perceptive speech made by Donald C. Platten, vice president of a New York bank (and a volunteer in a number of nonprofit organizations), to an association of fund-raising directors in New York, I discovered some observations on that topic. I have summarized here what I believe are the four highlights of Platten's address:

1. Soon after the volunteer has been recruited, you should be able to identify the factors that motivated his or her agreement to serve. (*Author's Note:* These motivating factors are often revealed during the recruitment process.)
2. Platten commented that "unlike babies, volunteers are made, not born." That is, volunteers must be treated gently, praised often, and continually trained—working toward the day when they begin to generate ideas. (*Author's Note:* The exceptions to this are the volunteers who come

into the organization already highly motivated, with solid experience and expertise gained through past leadership roles in other organizations and/or through their professional or business careers.)

3. A time will always come when a volunteer's energy, enthusiasm, and motivation begin to lag. When this occurs, the challenge is yours to regenerate and maintain his or her interest and enthusiasm. (*Author's Note:* It is also your challenge to design ways of preventing this lag whenever possible and to take remedial action at the earliest sign of trouble.)

4. One way of keeping the volunteer working effectively is to show him or her that there is an ongoing infusion of new faces in the organization. There is nothing quite so discouraging as seeing only the same old faces, looking a little less dedicated and a little more tired. (*Author's Note:* You should be careful not to replace "old faces" who are performing effectively and enthusiastically—and who also have the additional dimension of on-the-job experience.)

A broader statement of the volunteer's bill of rights was made back in 1962 before a site conference of social workers in the northwest by a director of volunteers of The American Red Cross. The ten "rights" appear just as valid today as they were twenty years ago:

1. The right to be treated as a coworker, not just free help, not as a prima donna.
2. The right to suitable assignments with consideration for personal preference, temperament, life experience, education, and employment background.
3. The right to know as much as possible about the organization—its policies, its people, its programs.
4. The right to training for the job.
5. The right to continuing education on the job, information about new developments, training for greater responsibility.
6. The right to sound guidance and direction from someone who is experienced and has the time to invest in giving guidance.

7. The right to a place to work, an orderly designated place worthy of the job to be done.
8. The right to promotion and a variety of experiences.
9. The right to be heard, to have a part in planning.
10. The right to recognition in the form of promotion, awards, day-by-day expression of appreciation, and treatment as a bonafide co-worker.

That is a reasonable statement of the rights of the volunteer. The extent to which it is recognized and fulfilled will determine the continuing strength of volunteerism.

VOLUNTEER RECRUITMENT

*T*he first step in developing an effective force of volunteers is to consider the following prerecruitment activities:

1. Determine the number of prospects that you are planning to contact.
2. Determine the number of volunteers needed to contact these prospects. Decide how many prospects will be assigned to each solicitor, recognizing that major gifts workers normally are assigned fewer prospects than residential campaign workers.
3. Identify all of your sources of volunteers such as board members, former volunteers, alumni, past donors, persons who have used your services, and friends.
4. Determine who your best recruiters might be, and what kind of approach might be most effective.
    A. *Recommended combinations to enlist the general campaign chairperson:* Chairperson of the governing board, chairperson of the board development committee, president or CEO, chief development officer.
    B. *Recommended combinations to enlist the chairperson of the working divisions:* General campaign chairperson and others of his or her own selection.
    C. *Recommended combinations to enlist the chairpersons of districts or groups:* Division chairperson and others of his or her own selection.

D. *Recommended combination to enlist the workers (solicitors):* District or group chairperson and others of his or her own selection.

SELECTING TOP LEADERSHIP

After all of the prerecruiting activities have been completed, the next, and critically important, step is the selection and recruitment of top leadership, beginning with the general campaign chairperson. Obviously, this should be someone who holds a high position in the business or social life of the community, but this in itself is not sufficient. The general chairperson must have the willingness and the time to work. A prominent name on a letterhead alone will not attract support.

A general campaign chairperson must lead, must inspire by example, and must be a pacesetter, both in the quality of the leadership team that he or she forms, and in the size and number of pacesetting contributions that he or she is able to generate. That familiar expression, "the speed of the boss is the speed of the game," still applies. The same criteria should hold true (although on a smaller scale) for volunteers at all levels of the campaign organization.

Whenever possible, vice-chairpersons should be recruited by the chairperson of the general campaign or major campaign divisions for the following reasons:

1. If the chairperson is unavailable during the campaign, the duties of the office can be performed by the vice-chairperson without interruption. Otherwise, the campaign must proceed without its top volunteer leader at the helm.
2. A vice-chairperson can provide valuable assistance to the chairperson in the numerous issues, events, and interactions that need attention throughout the campaign.

3. Some organizations now have adopted a procedure of filling the vice-chairperson position with the person who has been designated to serve as general chairperson of the next year's campaign. This not only provides the chairperson with a capable deputy, but also gives that individual valuable experience in the operation of that office.

THE RECRUITMENT PROCESS

During the recruitment process, all volunteers should receive the following information:

1. A written description of the specific duties and responsibilities of the position for which they were recruited, including attending appropriate orientation sessions.
2. A copy of the Volunteer Workers Handbook, which contains detailed instructions designed to provide workers with reliable guidelines for the accomplishment of their missions in an orderly and uniform manner.
3. An organization chart, indicating their respective positions in the overall operation, and giving them a broad picture of the entire campaign.
4. A memorandum informing them of the guidance and assistance available from the development staff, other volunteer leaders, and board members.
5. A statement to the effect that nonreimbursed out-of-pocket expenses incurred in connection with the performance of volunteers' duties may be deducted as "contributions" on their federal income tax returns. This includes allowable mileage or the actual cost of gas and oil (for those driving to and from the volunteer work), parking fees, tolls, travel expenses, and meals. Receipts, cancelled checks, or other reliable written records should be kept showing the name of the organization, the date and amount of the expenditures, and the nature of the expenses.

The recruitment process must be conducted on a face-to-face basis, and may require more than one meeting. Decide in advance who will attend the first meeting, who will attend the second meeting, who will lead the discussions, and what the major points of emphasis will be. Decide also where these meetings should be held.

At some point during the recruitment process, leadership candidates should visit your organization, tour your facilities, and see your programs in action.

CONFIRMING AND ANNOUNCING APPOINTMENTS

As soon as a volunteer has accepted a position in your campaign, the appointment should be reported to campaign headquarters and a letter of confirmation issued with the signature of the general campaign chairperson. Press releases announcing the enrollment of all volunteers should be sent to local newspapers, hometown newspapers, and other appropriate publications, including your own.

What You Can Do Tomorrow:
Recruitment of Volunteer Leadership

1. Assemble pertinent data from the evaluation process of the last campaign and from your own records, which would identify promising candidates for leadership positions, some to repeat their roles and others to be asked to assume higher volunteer positions.
2. Identify candidates for volunteer leadership from other traditional sources, including members of the governing board and past and present users of your services.
3. Make a rough draft of all of your recommendations, including background information, for subsequent presentation to and discussion with the chairperson of your governing board.

ORIENTATION OF VOLUNTEERS

*T*he objectives of volunteer orientation are to inform and to motivate. I have attended numerous orientation meetings, both as a volunteer and as a guest, where information in large quantities was provided about the campaign, about the organization's history, programs, and objectives, about the ways in which support can be given, about ways in which support can be induced, and other useful bits of campaign strategy. My criticism of most of these meetings centers around a lack of dialogue between the presenters and the trainees, and a failure to involve the talents of volunteers whose performance in past campaigns or whose positions in business or professional life indicate that they have training skills valuable to the group.

Those who plan orientation meetings should allow ample time for audience feedback. Much of the material presented could be mailed to volunteers in advance of the meeting for their review and subsequent comments. (Volunteers should receive written basic information about the organization, the campaign, and their specific assignments at the time of recruitment.)

Obviously, volunteers will be more likely to attend meetings where they will have an opportunity to participate. Also, volunteers who have proven records of excellence should be used as presenters, together with trained staff.

ORIENTATION AS TRAINING

Poor or inadequate orientation of volunteers is a major cause of campaign failure. With rare exception volunteers need to be "trained," although they tend to resist the term. Most volunteers need knowledge about campaigning in general, solicitation skills and techniques such as how to request prospects to "join them" in supporting the important work of your organization, and in how to deal with traditional excuses such as "too many campaigns," "giving budget is exhausted," and others that signal a lack of interest.

Some organizations have effectively helped volunteers to acquire campaign skills—and also enlivened their orientation meetings—by presenting skits first demonstrating "how not to approach a prospect" and then the recommended and proven ways of successful solicitation. Volunteers or celebrity guests should be selected as "the players," with staff acting as directors.

You and your colleagues should be alert to any of the many other ways of effectively orienting and motivating your volunteers, and apply those methods in your programs. And while you are devising methods of making your orientation meetings interesting, unique, and meaningful, do not overlook the creature comforts of your volunteers: a pleasant, uncrowded, well-ventilated, well-lit, and easily accessible meeting site, good parking accommodations including reimbursing volunteers for parking fees or arranging with a nearby parking garage to be billed for the volunteers' parking charges, a convenient time of day for the meeting, appropriate refreshments, and, above all, the opportunity to be introduced and to speak.

ASSIGNMENT OF PROSPECTS

*T*he assignment of prospects, a key element in any fund-raising operation, often is handled carelessly, or ignored, resulting in major prospects and able volunteers being grossly mismatched.

The majority of successful campaigns incorporate into their planning mandatory meetings of solicitors (by group), held expressly for the purpose of allowing them to select prospects rather than having prospects assigned to them indiscriminately. At these meetings, lists of prospects are distributed to each solicitor, who indicates preferred prospects as the names of the prospects are read aloud. In cases where more than one solicitor chooses the same prospect, each identifies his or her relationship to the prospect, then the chairperson decides who should receive the assignment.

After this process has been completed, the unselected prospects are divided among the workers who have not selected their quota. Here again, these workers can choose unsolicited prospects before mandatory assignments are made.

When workers are not able to attend an assignment meeting, lists of remaining prospects are sent to them for selection and return, so that duplicate selections can be resolved at campaign headquarters. The workers then receive their official assignment lists.

Workers should be cautioned to contact only those prospects that have been assigned to them. Duplicate calls on the same prospect can be embarrassing and confusing.

Instances of perfect matchups between workers and prospects are rare, but the selection process obviously increases the chances for success over the arbitrary assignment method.

VOLUNTEER/STAFF RELATIONS

*T*he volunteer force and the staff have important and distinctive roles in the operation of any good fund-raising program. Both the responsibilities and differences of these two major players should be clearly defined, understood, and accepted by all concerned. Failure to do this often results in confusion and a lack of harmony, and easily could jeopardize the success of the entire campaign.

The staff members do most of their important work behind the scenes, planning, advising, and giving direction to the volunteer force when necessary. The volunteers, on the other hand, are out on the firing line, recruiting and supervising other volunteers, and making the requests for contributions. They are the ones who are most visible, the people who conduct and make the speeches at kickoffs and at report meetings, and the people whom you see and read about in the media. The exceptions to this are college and university presidents and chief executive officers of other nonprofit organizations. Briefly stated:

VOLUNTEERS ESTABLISH POLICIES
STAFF MEMBERS EXECUTE POLICIES

or

VOLUNTEERS LEAD
STAFF MEMBERS MANAGE—AND SERVE

While the campaign chairperson (volunteer) and the campaign director (staff) form the traditional leadership partnership, each heads his or her own team. The role of each may vary slightly among different organizations, but here is a breakdown of responsibilities that can be applied to staff and volunteers in any setting.

ROLE AND RESPONSIBILITIES OF THE CAMPAIGN DIRECTOR (STAFF):

(Sometimes referred to as vice president for development, vice president or director of income development, campaign manager, etc.)

The Campaign Director:

1. Prepares the campaign plan for presentation to the campaign chairperson for input, appropriate revision, and approval. The plan should include goals and quotas, tables of organization, an operational timetable, a budget, and a determination of the number of staff and volunteers needed with definitions of their job responsibilities, identification of prospects, campaign materials, special events, etc.
2. Develops the case statement (unless the chief executive officer chooses to do this).
3. Assists the chairperson of the board and/or chairperson of the campaign committee of the board (also referred to as the board development committee or council) in the selection and recruitment of the general campaign chairperson.
4. Assists the general campaign chairperson and all subsequent levels of leadership in the selection and recruitment of all volunteers.
5. Sets up the campaign headquarters and an efficient record, accounting, and reporting system. Supervises planning and production of campaign materials.
6. Researches and develops prospect lists for all volunteers in the various divisions of the campaign organization, such as special gifts, business and industry, foundations, small businesses, residential, clubs and organizations, and alumni.
7. Organizes and supervises programs designed to train, orient, and motivate volunteers throughout the campaign.
8. Assists the campaign leaders in keeping the campaign on schedule.
9. Ensures that proper acknowledgment is made for all contributions of money, for volunteer service, for media

support, and for endorsements from public officials in the form of proclamations, appearances, etc.

10. Evaluates the entire campaign effort.

RESPONSIBILITIES OF THE CAMPAIGN CHAIRPERSON (VOLUNTEER):

The Campaign Chairperson:

1. Reviews the campaign plan and the case statement, makes appropriate revisions where necessary (and in keeping with organizational policies), and gives final approval.
2. Enrolls leaders at lower echelons and assists them in their recruitment efforts.
3. Chairs all official campaign functions (kickoffs, report meetings, special events, orientation and training meetings, etc.)
4. Supervises all solicitation activities, through campaign channels, using staff support when advisable, helpful, or necessary.
5. Makes appropriate appearances on television and radio, gives interviews to newspaper reporters, and appears at news conferences when necessary.
6. Works with the campaign director to maintain strict adherence to operational timetables and to oversee remedial action to correct any weaknesses or breakdowns that may occur at any stage of the campaign.
7. Sets the standard for giving by making a substantial pace-setting contribution early in the campaign.
8. Provides an evaluation of the campaign and makes recommendations for the following year.

SUPPORTING VOLUNTEERS

As a final note, I want to share with you some highlights from a fine speech entitled, "What a Volunteer Expects of Staff," delivered to the staff of the American Cancer Society's Illinois Division on June 1, 1961, by Charles W. Ebersold, Vice President–Merchandising, Illinois Bell Telephone Company, and State Chairman of the 1961 record-breaking Crusade of the American Cancer Society. (I had the privilege of being there as State Campaign Director.) Although this was about 30 years ago, Mr. Ebersold's insights are just as appropriate today as they were then.

In his speech, Mr. Ebersold emphasized three major means by which staff can support volunteers:

1. *Accurate, complete, and readily available facts:* Specifically, a status report of each campaign unit on the first day of the campaign followed by (at least) weekly progress reports indicating where things are going well and where they are not.
2. *Comprehensive organizational charts:* These show volunteer and staff job levels, job descriptions and responsibilities, and geographic service areas.
3. *"Perfection" in printed materials:* When a business executive volunteers, the reputation of his or her company, as well as the volunteer's own, is at stake. Accordingly, items poorly prepared by staff (letters, advertisements, brochures, etc.) cast doubt on the total capability and integrity of both the organization and the company that the volunteer represents.

Mr. Ebersold also urged that discussions between volunteer and staff regarding expectations of each be considered by every organization.

DEVELOPMENT OFFICER PROFILE

Many articles have been written that profile the effective volunteer, and well they should, because the volunteer is at the heart and helm of every fund-raising operation of any quality and substance. Profiles of development officers, however, rarely appear in print, and therefore volunteers and other staff members often lack understanding of how development officers are perceived by some corporate and foundation officials, and perhaps how best they should function.

For this reason, I was especially interested in reading the remarks made by Edward C. Logelin, vice president–midwest of United States Steel Corporation at a development workshop held in Chicago in 1974, and sponsored by Gonser, Gerber, Tinker, Stuhr in which he describes how development officers are viewed by corporate and foundation officials in general and by him in particular. His comments describe an excellent role model for all development officers.

"Over the years in my capacity with U.S. Steel Corporation, I have had an opportunity to meet literally hundreds of development officers—some highly professional, some part-time, and some who were strictly amateur. As a would-be objective outsider, I would describe the requirements for a development officer as one-third salesmanship, one-third public relations, and one-third hope-springs-eternal."

Mr. Logelin goes on to describe common characteristics that mark the effective development officers he has observed, worked with, and listened to:

1. They have great faith in, and enthusiasm for, the organization they represent.
   They believe, as they meet each prospect, that they are about to offer him the greatest opportunity he has ever had to invest time, effort, or money in an outstanding endeavor.
2. They follow the first rules every salesman learns—know your product and know your prospect. The ability to answer any and every question the prospect may ask is important. So, too, is the candor to admit one doesn't know the answer when a new question arises. I'm using the word "prospect" loosely. It could mean a prospective board member, committee member or fund-raising volunteer, as well as possible corporate or foundation donor.
   Knowing the prospect is worth the time it takes for research. I'm always troubled when I am approached for a grant to an institution whose purposes are beyond the purview of the U.S. Steel Foundation. For

example, as a matter of policy, the U.S. Steel Foundation does not contribute to secondary education. The development officer who puts together a brochure and asks for an interview to present it has wasted his time and cost the institution precious promotional dollars.

3. They touch all bases. I have mentioned that I am not a part of the U.S. Steel Foundation, which is headquartered in Pittsburgh. Yet the vice president of the Foundation naturally will turn to local officers of the Corporation who are close to the community for their judgment as to the value of a specific proposal.

   By the same token, in those matters where corporate grants are involved, if I am approached, my first question is whether the local plant superintendent has been consulted. I think it is only human nature that a local representative who is by-passed by an institution will be less than ecstatic when he receives an internal request for an opinion.

4. They are proud of their organization, confident in their approach, but never arrogant or condescending. Recently a church organization with which I am familiar secured a new development officer. Within a few months he had alienated both the clerical and lay leadership of the congregation which was by far the largest contributor to the project. I believe that had he gone to that church for advice and counsel and with a real sense of sharing the financial problems, he would have received instant help.

   In another case, I was approached for a corporate gift by the president of a college whose philosophy I admired. I was receptive to working with him to prepare a presentation to the Foundation for a one-time grant. I was, that is, until he referred to the annual operating help his school had received in sneering tones, describing it as a tip, rather than a contribution. Since the annual gifts had amounted to $10,000 in a few years time, I ceased to be his ally.

CAMPAIGN PUBLICATIONS

*T*he number and nature of publications and forms necessary for a particular campaign vary with the nature and design of that campaign. However, a set of standard publications are used, in various combinations, in the majority of successful fund-raising operations. Consider and select those which may best match your needs:

1. *The Case Statement*, also known as the statement of the case, statement of objectives, etc.
2. *Basic Campaign Brochure*, containing information about the organization's history, structure, program, governing board, administration, budget, needs, and ways in which support can be given
3. *Handbook of Instructions*, for volunteer workers
4. *Forms for Reporting Contributions Received, Volunteers Enrolled*
5. *Contributions and Pledge Forms*
6. *Special Brochures or Pamphlets on Planned Gifts and Opportunities for Memorial and Special Occasion Giving*
7. *Campaign Newsletters and Special Reports*
8. *Fact Book or Fact Sheet About the Organization* or about a particular capital facility or program for which support is being sought
9. *Posters, Films, Exhibits, and other Promotional Material*

A word of caution: Before spending time and money on campaign materials, make sure that there is a real need for each item on your list, and that it will be used. Often, materials that seemed essential end up on a stockroom shelf.

Standard Campaign Contribution (Pledge) Card

In consideration of the gifts of others, I hereby
contribute the amount of $_____
for support of your programs:

Please designate my gift for:

_____ greatest need
_____ building fund
_____ endowment

Payment schedule:

_____ amount enclosed herewith
_____ equal annual payments over a 3-year period
_____ equal annual payments over a 5-year period

Contribution secured by:

_____

_____

_____
(date)

_____
(name)

_____
(address)

_____
(telephone number)

☐ I would like more information regarding opportunities for legacies and bequests.

What You Can Do Tomorrow:
Preparation of Campaign Materials

1. Call a special meeting of the appropriate members of your
   development and public relations staff for the following
   purposes:
   A. To review last year's materials and their evaluation by
      staff and volunteers to determine their suitability.

    B. To decide on any changes, deletions, or additions to any of the materials that were reviewed.

    C. To decide whether any new materials should be considered.

2. Begin to prepare all of the background summaries to send to each committee member well in advance of the meeting.

3. Prepare your own evaluation and recommendations for presentation at the meeting.

SECTION III

The

Campaign

THE COMPREHENSIVE DEVELOPMENT PROGRAM

*T*here appears to be widespread misunderstanding about the differences between a development program and a fund-raising campaign, how they relate to one another, and their respective advantages and disadvantages.

A development program is an ongoing program with specific immediate and long-range goals, and includes the following three major components, two of which actually are fund-raising campaigns:

1. The Annual Fund
2. The Capital Campaign
3. Planned Giving

Comprehensive development programs have certain advantages over traditional fund-raising campaigns. Development programs provide opportunities for multidimensional support, often from the same donors, including contributions to the annual fund, contributions to capital projects that are of special interest to the donor, and support through legacies and bequests of various kinds. This results in significant increases in the levels of giving because it enables the organization to capitalize on the interest shown by the donor in making the initial gift. While annual giving programs, capital campaigns, and planned giving programs are closely coordinated, each of these support areas interfaces with one another. This results not only in sharp increases in total gift income, but also helps to keep alive the public image, programs, and needs of the organization.

The chief advantage of the traditional fund-raising campaign lies in its ability to reach its goal within a shorter period of time. Its chief disadvantage is that, when the campaign is over, there is no ongoing fund-raising activity into which the fringe benefits, such as volunteer and donor interest, can be transferred.

Many organizations have been able to establish patterns of three-part giving among its governing board members, alumni leaders, and other key volunteers. Through their support of the annual fund and capital programs, and their commitments through planned giving, these leaders greatly influence increases in the commitments and total support from others.

Development programs should not be restricted to large organizations. Even the smallest organization may embark on a long-range comprehensive development program, the only difference being the dimensions of the component programs.

Every organization should accomplish the following four tasks:

1. Document its short- and long-range goals at least three years into the future.
2. Conduct an organized annual campaign or ongoing fund-raising for operational support.
3. Hold periodic campaigns for its capital and other special needs.
4. Establish planned giving programs, such as requesting that all members of the organizational family consider inclusion of the organization in their wills, and to consider other forms of legacy or bequest support; requesting major donors and other friends of the organization do the same.

In setting up a sound development program, keep in mind a number of underlying key factors that are prevalent in most of the successful operations:

- Workers and prospects for annual giving and capital campaigns often are drawn from other facets of the overall fund development program of the institution, so all of these facets must be kept active and viable.

- At the completion of the respective campaigns, most of the volunteer workers and prospects are returned to the facets from which they came and remain as productive sources of support for the organization.
- Donors who may have been making nominal annual gifts or who make nominal gifts in the first year of the capital campaign may be prospects for much larger gifts in the excitement and pressure of the campaign, and when specific objectives that are of interest to them are presented.
- Major gifts come most often from those who already are supporting the organization; therefore, the strengthening of the regular annual giving base represents an important cultivating vehicle for the entire development program.
- Not all prospective donors are interested in annual giving or capital programs (at a given time) and it is essential that they be provided with suitable outlets for their current interests, such as programmatic, operating, endowment, or legacies and bequests. Interests do change, however, and many donors eventually become prospects for contributions *instead of or in addition to* their previous giving patterns and commitments.
- Most donors prefer to contribute to organizations that already are well-supported or who show promise of attracting support. Accordingly, many prospects for major grants are especially impressed by an organization that can demonstrate strong internal support from its governing board members, alumni, women's board, associates, and other members of the organizational family.

DEVELOPMENT PROGRAM CHECKLIST

Check the following eleven characteristics of a successful development program and see how many apply to your fundraising operation:

1. The development program occupies a high priority in the organization's leadership structure. This is reflected in

the appointment of a board committee on development and the relative stature of the members appointed thereto.

2. The overall missions, objectives, and programs of the organization are well-defined, well-documented, and divided into short-range and long-range (at least three years) goals.

3. There is a written plan for a comprehensive development program designed to achieve the goals previously described. This development plan is communicated to everyone in the organization and contains a carefully constructed timetable of operations.

4. The development program is comprehensive and includes annual giving, capital programs, and planned (deferred) giving.

5. Development staff and volunteer leadership have established priorities so that time and effort are spent in areas of greatest return.

6. There are efficient systems for charting and reporting progress and problems to staff, volunteers, and donors on a regular basis. Reports of problems are accompanied by clear explanations, by appropriate leaders, of remedial measures that are being or will be taken.

7. The development program gives highest priority to the proper identification, cultivation, and procurement of major gifts, hopefully to raise at least 85 percent of the goal from 15 percent of the donors.

8. The development plan is based on personal contact and possesses a sense of excitement and a feeling of universality.

9. Proper recognition is given to everyone involved. This includes appropriate acknowledgment of contributions and volunteer service.

10. There is a mechanism for keeping all of the organization's publics informed of its progress on a year-round basis through periodic newsletters, bulletins, annual reports, and media features, etc.

11. Everyone involved at both staff and volunteer levels knows specifically what his or her duties are. These duties and responsibilities are clearly identified in writing.

If any of these elements are missing from your development program, they should be incorporated into your fund-raising operation as swiftly as possible because each of these "missing links" can be important to the success or failure of any campaign.

COMPREHENSIVE DEVELOPMENT PROGRAMS

The characteristics of the three components of comprehensive development programs (the annual fund, the capital campaign, and planned giving) are the topics of discussion for the remainder of this chapter.

I. The Annual Fund

The annual fund often is referred to as "annual giving," and can be conducted either on an ongoing basis throughout the year or through an intensive annual campaign within a shorter time frame, such as the American Cancer Society's crusade in April, the American Heart Association's campaign in February, and the United Way Campaigns.

The annual fund is the major source of support for current operations. It has been referred to as the cornerstone of a comprehensive development program.

But a well-organized and well-managed annual fund does much more than provide support for current operations. It brings many donors into the program for the first time, which helps to strengthen the base for both capital and planned giving programs. The annual fund also becomes an excellent source for the development of expanded giving. Many contributors to annual funds increase the size of their gifts as the goals and needs of the organization increase, and as they become more interested and more committed to the cause.

The annual fund is always an important source of future volunteers, including those who might be potential board members and campaign leaders. Many effective volunteers had their first contact with an organization when they were initially asked to contribute to its annual fund.

Whether your organization conducts an annual campaign or carries on year-round fund-raising, the following basic ground rules apply:

1. Set goals that are supported by strong programs, and show how these programs relate to the overall objectives of your organization.
2. Construct a campaign plan that has the input and approval of the board development committee and ultimately the full board, so that it becomes everyone's plan and not just the plan of the staff.
3. Demonstrate that top priority is given to the annual fund by the high quality of leadership that is recruited from the top on down through to the ranks of the all important solicitors.
4. Include all appropriate sources of support in your prospect lists: board members, corporations, foundations, clubs and organizations, alumni, parents, merchants, and other friends.
5. Establish a timetable of operations and follow it.
6. Establish personal solicitation as the basic method of contact.
7. Establish a sound procedure for records, reports, and acknowledgments of contributions and volunteer services.

Remember that, although the annual fund is a crucially important part of your total development program, there are two other major components that are of equal importance and that depend on the annual fund for much of their base. Accordingly, donors to the annual fund (and its volunteers) should be informed at an appropriate time and in appropriate ways of the opportunities for extending their support through the capital and planned giving programs of your organization.

II. The Capital Campaign

Capital campaigns are conducted whenever capital projects and other special needs arise. At one time annual giving was temporarily halted during the capital fund-raising period. At the present time, more and more capital campaigns are conducted successfully simultaneously with the annual fund.

Careful preparation for the capital campaign can well determine the success or failure of the operation. Many capital campaigns are launched prematurely, and fail.

First, you must clearly define your objectives. If a new building is needed, you must be able to provide a full and detailed description of the facility and a clear definition of the programs that will be carried on within its walls.

The other basic elements of a successful capital campaign are similar to those that are required for an annual fund operation. These five are of paramount importance, and worth repeating:

1. A clear, well-written case statement.
2. Top quality volunteer leadership to head the campaign and its major divisions. Do not overlook volunteers who performed well in your annual fund campaigns.
3. An adequate budget with provisions for additional staff and all of the other traditional campaign essentials.
4. A sufficient number of well-researched and carefully rated prospects.
5. An appropriate gift table as described in detail in the chapter on standards of giving in Section II.

Because of the required intensity of a capital campaign, a timetable which schedules every step and detail of the operation must be carefully followed. It is the joint responsibility of the general campaign chairperson and the staff campaign director to ensure that this is done.

Campaign Materials. In addition to the traditional basic materials used in annual campaigns, workers in a capital campaign should be equipped with the following items:

1. Artists' renderings of the buildings and the rooms available for commemorative gift naming. These should appear in the capital brochure. Some prospects like to see blueprints, so this also would be a useful item to have.
2. Shopping lists of gift opportunities, showing the gift amounts necessary to have certain units within the building (floors, wings, rooms, etc.), or the building itself, named in accordance with the donor's wishes. Samples

(photographs) of plaques and other methods of designation should also be provided.

Special Events. Capital campaigns provide opportunities for dramatic special events that can lend great impact to the operation. Examples are groundbreaking, "topping," and dedication ceremonies not only for the building but also for named units such as libraries, classrooms, laboratories, auditoriums, and gymnasiums.

You may also be able to request proclamations from governors, mayors, and other public officials, which newspapers generally are willing to announce, and which make interesting news items for your internal publications.

Letters expressing the good wishes of the President of the United States have been secured in the past in response to requests by appropriate congressmen and other influential individuals.

You should consider enlisting the cooperation and support of prominent individuals from the fields of politics, entertainment, and sports. These public figures frequently are very receptive to requests for their appearance at kickoffs, report meetings, and news conferences.

The creation of other suitable ways to maintain the interest and enthusiasm of campaign workers should be the responsibility of a publicity and special events committee headed by a chairperson appointed by the general campaign chairperson.

III. Planned Giving

One of the greatest American ideas is that it is wise and good for men and women to leave a part of their estates to charitable, health, welfare, educational, and cultural organizations.

Legacies and bequests have become increasingly important sources of income, encouraged by favorable state and federal tax structures. Many nonprofit organizations, both large and small, now include planned giving as a regular part of their fund development programs. Although these programs generally do not produce quick results, many "surprises" have been reported by organizations along the way.

An example of this happened at a small college when an alumnus, after receiving a number of planned gift mailings, contacted the college and indicated his desire to make an appropriate planned gift. Approximately two weeks after his initial contact, he donated $275,000 worth of stock, and received from the college a combined annuity contract and living trust agreement which would nearly double his after-tax income for the rest of his life. In addition, he had the satisfaction of knowing that a dormitory already under construction would bear his name.

The term "planned giving" means different things to different people, and one finds a variety of definitions and applications of planned giving programs that are in effect today.

Robert A. Wiegand, attorney, former vice president in the trust department of the Continental Bank of Chicago and former director of Planned Giving at Lake Forest College, defined planned gifts as "major gifts which fit a particular donor's tax, financial, and estate planning needs." He made the following observations from his extensive experience in the field:

> Most prospective donors do not come forward with a particular kind of planned gift in mind. The process of determining the most appropriate form of gift offers the planned giving specialist important opportunities and responsibilities. His or her understanding of the full range of possibilities is therefore a crucial element in the successful search for such gifts.
>
> The planned giving process has the potential of becoming an extremely important public service vehicle for friends and donors of the institution. How many times has the routine personal contact of the planned giving officer led to the timely preparation of a will or trust agreement? Too often, potential donors are troubled by the process of finding an attorney or advisor, and unsure of themselves in making decisions about the ultimate disposition of their estates. A thoughtful and professional planned giving representative from a charitable organization may well be in the best position to recommend an experienced lawyer or quality trust company to

ensure that decisions are made and documents prepared. Out of this process comes the planned gift for the charitable organization.

The planned giving program should be organized and conducted under the direction of an appropriate committee of the governing board. Whenever possible, this committee should include individuals who have necessary expertise and influence in related fields such as law, trust management, estate planning, accounting, and insurance. The committee should meet at intervals agreed upon by the chairperson and its members.

While the staff appropriately directs the day-to-day activities of the program, overall guidance should come from the planned giving committee. The program should be low-key and soft-sell. People properly consider the distribution of their estates to be their own business and will usually resent anyone telling them how they should dispose of any part of it.

The operational plan should be simple and aimed at cultivating the interest and support of two principal groups. The first consists of board members, alumni, volunteers, and other members of the organizational family. The second group is broader and includes the following:

- Past donors
- Individuals who have been helped by the organization
- Special prospects identified by members of the planned giving committee of the board, by other board members, or by the staff
- Trust departments of major banks
- Trust or estate planning departments of major law firms
- Accounting firms
- Large insurance companies

Records. The development officer should establish a system of records that will ensure the collection and accessibility of information pertaining to participants and prospects in the program. Mechanical details differ with the institution and will depend to a great extent on the size and sophistication of the development department.

Cultivation. Although personal contact is the most effective way of communicating with every planned gift prospect, the limitations of time and manpower make this impossible. For this reason, the following plan is recommended:

1. Prepare a special planned giving pamphlet at intervals of six months and mail it with a cover letter *to all prospects*. The pamphlet should be planned with the participation of committee members to include appropriate information about the organization's programs, commemorative gift opportunities, and news about the planned giving program, such as progress and gifts received. The pamphlet also should include explanations of the more common kinds of planned gifts that are made and samples of wording that can be used by donors in making these gifts. (Sample forms appear at the end of this chapter.) The letters accompanying the pamphlets should be prepared by or with members of the committee. They should be individually typed, signed, and stamped. Form letters will not receive necessary attention.
2. Hold periodic (annual) meetings or seminars for selected prospects designed to inform them about programs, objectives, and planned gift opportunities, and to motivate them to act. Special meetings should be planned for attorneys, trust officers, accountants, and insurance executives.
3. Arrange personal one-on-one visits to selected prospects by appropriate committee members, accompanied by staff as necessary.
4. Ask the planned giving committee members for recommendations about other actions.

The Long-range View. The most successful planned giving programs usually begin at a modest level and gradually expand. Quick results are seldom realized. However, the systematic cultivation of planned giving prospects, including attorneys, trust officers, bankers, estate planning counselors, and insurance representatives, will eventually pay off. You should not become discouraged when your efforts appear to be unproductive and (under the pressure of more urgent duties) neglect the continued cultivation of your prospects. Often golden opportunities for substantial additional support are lost through impatience, indifference, or neglect. Patience is the name of the game.

Suggested Forms. A primary objective of an organization's planned giving program is to ensure, insofar as possible, that the purposes of gifts and bequest be flexible and of maximum use to the institution's long-range plans and needs. Sample forms for making gifts and bequests to the institution are not only valuable tools in this endeavor, but also provide the donor's attorney with such information as the institution's correct legal name and address. Accordingly, forms which may be used in making certain common kinds of planned gifts are suggested below.

Testamentary Bequest. A testamentary bequest is one which passes at the time of the estate settlement directly to the charity for its immediate use and employment. The common methods for specifying testamentary bequests include:

- An exact dollar amount.
- A fraction or percentage of the total estate, such as one-half or 50 percent.
- A fraction or all of the residuary estate—that part of the estate that is left after deduction of all expenses, debts, taxes, and specific bequests.
- Specific property, as, for example, a house, specified real estate or works of art, specified securities, or jewelry.

A charitable bequest under the terms of the will is fully deductible from the adjusted gross estate in arriving at the taxable estate. Furthermore, the tax savings is proportionately larger in relation to the total tax due than the gift is in relation to the total estate. Because federal estate tax rates are progressive, property which the charitable bequest removes from the taxable estate would otherwise have been taxed at the highest rate.

Here are some examples of wording for legal forms that may be used in making unrestricted and restricted testamentary bequests:

1. *Testamentary bequest, unrestricted, as to purpose.*

   "I give, and bequeath, to (legal name of institutions), a not-for-profit corporation duly existing under the laws of the State of (state of incorporation) and located at (legal address of institution) _____ dollars (or property, securities, etc., as described below), to be used as the Trustees of (name of institution) may direct."

2. *Testamentary bequest to establish endowment fund with income (or other purpose specified by testator)—(a) unrestricted, or (b) restricted.*

   "I give, and bequeath, to (legal name of institution), a not-for-profit corporation duly existing under the laws of the State of (state of incorporation) and located at (legal address of institution) _____ dollars (or property, securities, etc., as described below), to constitute the (name of endowment) Fund. This Fund shall be kept invested by the Trustees of (legal name of institution) and the annual income thereof utilized—

   (a) as the trustees may direct.

   (b) for (description of restricted purpose specified by testator—i.e., scholarships, faculty compensation, library, etc.).

A Living Trust.   A living trust can be established naming your organization as the beneficiary of either principal or income from the trust. A life income trust can be set up where the donor transfers money, securities, or other property to a trustee, who pays the income to the donor for life, after which the principal is turned over to the beneficiary.

ADVANTAGES OF A LIVING TRUST:

1. To the donor:

A deferred gift made during the donor's lifetime, again in addition to the personal satisfaction derived, can have important income tax and estate tax implications. Such a gift in many cases can actually increase the donor's spendable income during his lifetime.

2. To the recipient:

The obvious advantage to the charitable organization of a lifetime gift compared to a bequest is that a lifetime gift is irrevocable, while a will can be changed. Another advantage is that such gifts enable the recipient to make long-range plans. Institutions with enough retained income contracts, trusts, and annuities in force can predict actuarily how much principal will become available during various periods of time in the future. As with bequests, the donor's greater involvement after making the first gift can be very important. One gift often can lead to more in the future.

A Gift Annuity.   A gift annuity is an agreement between a gift-supported institution and a donor, whereby the donor contributes a given sum of cash, securities, or other property in return for an agreement on the part of the institution to pay the donor, and a surviving beneficiary if desired, a fixed income for life. The principal is released absolutely to the institution upon the death of the surviving beneficiary.

A Gift of Life Insurance.   A gift of a life insurance policy, although essentially a deferred gift, has special advantages for the charitable beneficiary.

1. The assignment procedure is simple, with a form usually readily obtainable from the insurer, and completed upon delivery of the policy. Neither a trust, nor a provision in a will, nor investment supervision is necessary.
2. The amount the charity is to receive is certain and not subject to delay caused by administration of an estate or challenge to a will.
3. Even before the policy matures, the charity can use accumulated cash values or borrow against it.
4. As assignee, the institution has the right, should the donor cease paying premiums, to (a) continue the premiums; (b) obtain the cash surrender value; (c) purchase a paid-up or term policy for the then adjusted terminal reserve value of the original policy.

Outright Gifts. Many planned gifts are made outright. Actually, one major difference between a planned gift and a traditional contribution is that the latter is made generally in response to (and at the time of) a campaign request.

Planned giving literature should include the three different categories of outright gifts that can be made and the tax deductibility factor in each. These are summarized below:

1. **Gifts of Cash**—(the most popular gift): The date of the gift is considered to be the date on which it was hand delivered or mailed. The entire amount of the gift is deductible up to 50 percent of the donor's adjusted gross income. Any excess can be carried over for five years.

2. **Gifts of Appreciated Property** such as appreciated securities and real estate (long-term capital gain property): Here the donor is entitled to a tax deduction of the full fair market value of the gift up to 30 percent of the donor's adjusted gross income. Amounts in excess of 30 percent can be carried forward for up to five years.

3. **Gifts of Tangible Personal Property** such as jewelry, books, art objects, stamps and coin collections, antiques: If the use of the contributed item is related to the exempt purposes of the recipient organization (books to a library) then the donor is entitled to a tax deduction for its full market value, subject to legal limitations. If the use of the contributed item is not related to the exempt purposes of the recipient organization, but is intended for the recipient to sell and keep the proceeds, then the donor is entitled to a tax deduction only on his or her cost basis in the contributed item. Finally, if someone donates an item of personal property that he or she created (a painter of a donated portrait or landscape), the tax deduction is limited to the actual production cost.

Computerized Programs. Any discussion of planned giving would be incomplete if it failed to include ways in which computerized programs can provide quick and valuable assistance. My friend Bob Wiegand has had a great deal of experience in this area and has made the following recommendations of how to "incorporate a valuable easy-to-use and inexpensive computer program for your operation":

> In my opinion, the acquisition and use of a computer program is an invaluable part of the planned giving program. I believe this is true even for the small charitable organization operating with a limited budget.
>
> There are several computer companies which offer programs and carefully prepared user manuals at moderate prices. Some companies also offer, without additional charge, the services of a planned giving consultant. All of the companies can easily determine the kind of computer which is required for the optimum use of the software containing the planned giving program.
>
> The typical computer program incorporates most, if not all, of the following planned giving options:
>
> - Charitable Remainder Annuity Trust
> - Charitable Remainder Unitrust
> - Immediate Gift Annuity
> - Deferred Gift Annuity
> - Charitable Lead Annuity Trust
> - Charitable Lead Unitrust
> - Gift of a Farm or Residence
> - Pooled Income Fund
>
> Calculations for all of these options can be produced instantaneously. The detailed tax figures which produce the value are also available. The printout of the calculation, as well as the printout of a detailed gift explanation, will provide a charitable organization with most of the planned giving skills necessary to begin building this important category of giving.
>
> In addition to the calculations and explanations, the program has the capability of storing detailed prospect-donor information for literally hundreds of names. For many organizations, this single feature may justify the entire system.

An additional important benefit from a computer program for planned giving is the potential for training office staff members in the process.

I believe that relatively inexperienced people who have a minimal understanding of the use of computers can quickly learn to use the computer planned giving program.

Keeping the Planned Giving Program on Track. This 13-point checklist may help you to ensure that your planned giving program is on track:

1. Does the program have the full and enthusiastic support of your board? Has a planned giving committee of the board been appointed? Are board members recommending prospects and are they themselves participating in some meaningful way?
2. Do you offer donors opportunities to establish permanent memorials in their names or in the names of others? Are you keeping everyone informed of planned gift opportunities at your organization?
3. Does your program offer the donor a variety of planned giving methods?
4. Do you have a competent staff member to direct your planned giving program?
5. Do you have an established procedure for drawing up and closing a planned gift contract and for the subsequent management of annuity, trust, life income, and other funds?
6. Does the board receive a progress report at each meeting by the chairman of the planned giving committee?
7. Do you have a planned giving brochure for cultivation mailings and for the use of committee members in contacting prospective major donors?
8. Are personal calls being made to selected prospects and are reports of these calls made to the committee chairperson and staff director?
9. Is your special planned giving publication sent out (at least) annually to your entire prospect list?

10. Do you keep careful records to ensure compliance with the provisions of planned gifts?
11. Do you have annual informational luncheons (or other types of meetings) for attorneys, trust officers, accountants, insurance executives, and other investment advisors to keep them informed of your progress and your current funding needs?
12. Do you request permission from planned gift donors to recognize their support at meetings, in news releases, and/or in your newsletters, annual reports, or other publications?
13. Do you acknowledge in a meaningful way the receipt of planned gifts and the efforts of volunteers in your planned gifts programs?

SOLICITING MAJOR GIFTS FROM INDIVIDUALS

Major gifts can mean different things to different people depending on the relative size of their respective organizations. There are no standard dollar parameters to use as guidelines for everyone. When we refer to major gifts, we're really talking about thoughtful, proportionate gifts, with heavy emphasis on the word *proportionate*. This definition clearly separates solicitation of major gifts from a collection of funds which is designed to secure coverage with no serious attempt made to influence the size of the contributions.

Before major gifts can be solicited successfully, the prospective donors must be carefully identified, rated, cultivated, and assigned to a carefully chosen and exceptionally well-oriented volunteer. This must be a systematic effort, requiring the cooperation and participation of the governing board, the president or chief executive officer, the chief development officer, other administrators, and the most able volunteers in the organization.

More often than not, more than one of these individuals are involved in major gift solicitation.

This must be a team effort, and each member of the team should play a specific role in the operation. The following sets of suggested responsibilities are general and can be applied to any organization.

THE DEVELOPMENT DIRECTOR

1. Advises and guides the general campaign chairperson in the appointment of a major gifts committee chairperson,

and then assists that committee chairperson in the recruitment of committee members from the highest levels of the organization's leadership, including the governing board, president, and key volunteers.

2. Directs or performs the research necessary to identify major gifts prospects, and oversees the rating of each one, so that information is developed regarding financial ability, past and present relationships with the organization, past record of giving to other causes, and any other information that might guide and assist the solicitors in obtaining thoughtful, proportionate contributions.

3. Oversees the assignment of each prospect to the worker who is most likely to be effective. This is best done in a meeting or series of meetings with members of the major gifts committee so that they can participate in an assignment process.

4. Works with the campaign leadership, including the major gifts committee chairperson in establishing an operational timetable, including report meetings and a reporting system between meetings, so that the program can be tightly controlled.

5. Keeps the committee chairperson informed daily of all contributions or pledges received, and/or negative responses from prospects, as reported by the solicitors.

BOARD MEMBERS

Board members, by their very presence on the board, help to enhance the organization's credibility, and this is extremely important.

1. Board members should establish necessary priorities of need within the organization.

2. The more affluent board members should agree to accept responsibility for certain numbers of prospects of their own choosing, contacting them alone or accompanied by others, such as presidents, CEOs, other board members, or the director of development.

3. Prior to making these contacts, the board members should make their own contributions.

4. Board members should identify other major gifts prospects and assist in their cultivation and solicitation.

5. Board members should be alert to opportunities to express their appreciation to major gift donors, and to create other opportunities where none exist, such as by inviting donors to private thank-you luncheons or dinners, or inviting them to be guests at appropriate organizational functions, special events, and social events.

6. Accordingly, present board members should consider individuals with these combined qualities when selecting candidates for additions to the board.

PRESIDENT OR CHIEF EXECUTIVE OFFICERS

The president's or chief executive officer's role in fund-raising has been defined in the sample campaign master plan which is featured in Appendix A in this book. Three key responsibilities that the president must carry out are vital to the success of the major gifts operation.

1. The president must be willing to accept major gifts prospects of his or her own choosing, cultivate their interests by involving them in appropriate organizational activities (and in a variety of other ways), and then make the request for support, either alone or accompanied by others.

2. The president must be available to accompany board members and/or campaign volunteers on calls where his or her presence is needed as the chief resource and spokesperson for the organization.

3. The president should initiate the preparation and submission of proposals that match the special interests of prospective major donors.

RESEARCH AND RATING

The prospective donor is the object of all of the preparation, organization, and strategy of the major gifts operation. Prospect research in a major gifts program must be comprehensive, thorough, and should extend beyond the traditional parameters of identity, special interests, past giving records, ability to give in large amounts, and other traditional relevant information. The major key to success lies in the identification of the best person, or persons, to cultivate and solicit the prospect.

Rating of every major prospect is an important initial step in helping to secure the type of proportionate giving necessary to the success of your campaign. The data produced in the rating process enables the organization to assign gift potentials to each prospect. This, in turn, provides a starting point in seeking the sizes and number of gifts necessary to achieve the desired result of 85 percent of goal from 15 percent of donors.

Prospect research data generally is valuable for a number of reasons:

1. It helps to guide your organization in determining the types and numbers of cultivating activities that would be appropriate and effective.
2. It helps your organization to know what the best approach and the best points of emphasis should be in each presentation.
3. Finally, it helps to guide your organization in setting appropriate sights when deciding on what dollar figure should be incorporated into each request.

SOLICITING

Major gifts rarely are made during the first visit. Members of the major gifts team should decide with the solicitors who should be included in the second meeting, for example, a board member, the president, a development officer, or the organization's lawyer.

If a negative response is received, the major gifts team leaders should plan appropriate follow-up action. They must decide what the next move should be, and when and how it should be made. These decisions should be made with the following factors in mind:

1. Why was the prospect's response negative?
2. How did the solicitors and prospect end their discussion? Was there a door left open for a later call?
3. What type of follow-up would be most appropriate at this time and in this particular situation?
4. Finally, and of great importance, is the reality that a special gifts assignment may require many visits before the commitment is made.

FOLLOW-UP

Let's assume now that the major gift was made. What should be done to retain the donor's interest and to discharge faithfully the organization's responsibilities to the donor? This is a vital question, because the "after-gift follow through" is too often neglected or poorly accomplished.

First, the recipient organization must ensure that its records bear the correct name or names of the donor, the special purpose (if any) for which the gift was made, and any conditions that were agreed upon. Reports should be made on a regular basis, indicating that the gift is being used in accordance with the donor's wishes, and describing the important results that the funded project is producing.

The donor's generous interest and support should, of course, be acknowledged and recognized in every appropriate way possible. A number of specific approaches to this important action are described in the chapter on acknowledgment of contributions and volunteer services.

CHECKLIST

An effective major gifts effort requires year-round attention. The following nine-point checklist offers suggestions that may help you to keep your own program on track:

1. Does your organization have a major gifts committee that includes your president or chief executive officer, board members, other key volunteers, and a senior development officer?

2. Do you have a plan for cultivating prospect interest?
3. Is your case for support based on important programs and objectives that can be presented in a compelling way?
4. Do you maintain comprehensive prospect lists that are drawn from all appropriate sources (i.e., past donors, affluent members of your organizational family, others who are recommended by your board members, other volunteers, or your development officer as having reason to be interested in your program)?
5. Are all of your major prospects rated?
6. Do you try to involve your prospects as volunteers in programs which match their interests and abilities?
7. Are your acknowledgments of major gifts commensurate with their size and nature (such as public announcements in appropriate settings, multiple expressions of written and spoken gratitude, special events such as annual meetings or special donor recognition luncheons or dinners, and appropriate publicity, both external and internal)?
8. Is every major gift call carefully planned by a solicitor who is at least of equal stature with the prospect?
9. Has the solicitor made a gift prior to calling on the prospect?

MAJOR GIFTS ASSIGNMENT SHEET

The following suggested assignment sheet should be prepared for each prospect, in different colors and in quadruplicate.

1. Original copy for the solicitor
2. Second copy for office record
3. Third copy for team chairperson
4. Fourth copy for special gifts chairperson

It is important that the solicitor return the assignment sheet with information concerning the contact. These comments will be of value in preparation for the following year's campaign.

Major Gifts Assignment Sheet

Prospect: _____
Name

_____
Address

_____

Assigned to: _____
Name

_____
Address

_____

Date: _____

Prospect Record of Giving

Previous Year's Gift   *Rated 199_*

_____   _____
_____   _____
_____   _____
_____   _____

Remarks: _____

Comments on Contact: _____

_____

_____

_____

Guide for Special Gifts Workers

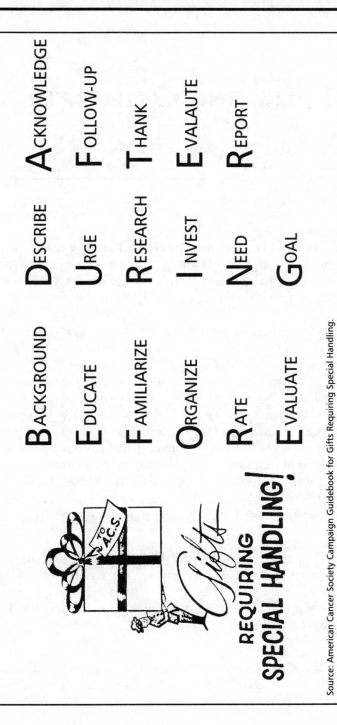

Background	Describe	Acknowledge
Educate	Urge	Follow-up
Familiarize	Research	Thank
Organize	Invest	Evalaute
Rate	Need	Report
Evaluate	Goal	

Gifts REQUIRING SPECIAL HANDLING!

Source: American Cancer Society Campaign Guidebook for Gifts Requiring Special Handling.

SOLICITING CORPORATIONS

*T*he corporate citizen has always had a major role in the sponsorship and support of philanthropic causes. This has not changed over the years, but the manner in which corporate philanthropy is conducted has become much more professional than ever before. An increasingly larger number of grants are project-oriented, rather than unrestricted; and the projects which receive the greatest support are those that match the corporation's objectives or interests.

Corporate grantmakers must account to management and to shareholders by showing a merger of the company's interests and needs with the charitable causes that receive support. This is especially important at a time when requests for grants almost always far outstrip the dollars available. The following statement is an excerpt from a lecture by William N. Clark, former executive director of the Robert R. McCormick Charitable Trust, delivered at a fund development seminar held by The Executive Service Corps of Chicago in June, 1989:

> Corporate Foundations must bear in mind the location and interests of customers, employees, and suppliers; and must bear the scrutiny of stockholders who may see a conflict between charitable works and funds available for dividends.

Mr. Clark went on to say that corporate foundations should not be condemned for this, but that they can do much good within these limitations.

TYPES OF CORPORATE GIFTS

Grants for Community Programs

Companies traditionally provide strong support to programs that address themselves to the improvement of the stability of the neighborhoods in which they have plants, offices, or stores. This support is manifested both by contributions and often by the provision of volunteers for various aspects of the program.

Contributions from Branch Operations

Many large corporations permit branches to make direct, modest contributions. In other instances, the parent company will support local causes recommended by branch executives.

Gifts in Kind

Gifts in kind are important additional sources of help. At modest cost to themselves, many companies can often supply expertise or merchandise of various kinds to nonprofit institutions at a fraction of market cost.

THINGS THAT MOST COMPANIES WANT TO KNOW

Most corporate grant guidelines require that answers to the following questions be included in all proposals.

1. To what extent does the asking organization duplicate the programs or services of others in the area?
2. Specifically, whom does the asking organization serve and are these services available to the entire community, rather than to only special groups?
3. Specifically, how does the asking organization serve?
4. What are the specific needs of the asking organization?
5. What other companies are supporting your organization?
6. What benefits would the corporate grant bring to its customers, its stockholders, and its employees?
7. What is the tax deductibility status of the asking organization?

NATURE OF CORPORATE GIVING

As the company size increases, the responsibility for administering contributions is delegated away from the chief executive officer and becomes more and more a functional activity of management, with subordinate executives taking over the task of receiving and evaluating contribution requests and recommending action to higher management.

Corporate Foundations

Frequently, foundations are set up to handle all or practically all of the charitable requests that the companies wish to consider. These foundations, for the most part, are simply extensions of the contributions programs of the companies which sponsor them.

In a number of instances, however, there is actually a division of grantmaking between the company and its own foundation, where certain types of programs are supported by the foundation, and others by the company. In the case of one national corporation, with many local branches, the company contributes to local causes through its local branches, and the foundation contributes to causes of regional or national scope.

Another basis for dividing the grantmaking between the company and its foundation is the period of time covered by the contributions commitment. When the commitment is for the current year only, it is usually handled as a company contribution; when it extends over several years, it is handled by the foundation.

Many companies maintain a division of responsibility with their foundations because of taxes. Corporate foundations operate under more restrictive tax regulations than do companies. Therefore, a company that allows all of its contributions to be handled through its foundation, is likely to find itself unable to support some of the programs that it would like to assist.

In instances where company policy directs that gifts be made to match those made by employees to certain approved charities, these matching grants can be made either by the company or its foundation.

COMPETITION FOR THE CORPORATE DOLLAR

As the needs of nonprofit organizations continue to rise, and corporations continue to be considered as major sources of support, competition for the corporate grant has become more and more intense. For example, a large midwestern corporate foundation recently reported that it receives approximately 3,000 requests a year and grants only 70.

The message is clear: Asking organizations must observe and carefully follow the guidelines that are described in company policy statements. Asking organizations also should do a better job in their program planning and in the preparation of their proposals. Consider the following observations made recently by a senior executive of a large corporation:

- Many proposals seem to lack innovative approaches to new problems. Companies are interested in problem solving, not just in dispensing money.
- Some organizations make multiple requests during the same fiscal year in spite of limitations that are clearly stated in published guidelines, indicating that only one proposal within the fiscal year from the same organization will be considered.
- Corporations are demanding more accountability from recipient organizations, in the form of periodic (semiannual or annual) progress reports, and assurances that the funds granted are being spent in accordance with the purposes intended by the grantmaking company.

CULTIVATION OF CORPORATE INTEREST

Every organization which seeks corporate support should maintain an ongoing program of cultivating the interest and understanding of local corporate executives. Here is a shopping list of cultivation activities. Select those which would be appropriate for your organization:

1. Ask certain corporate executives to serve on your governing board, or on appropriate advisory committees.
2. Generate and maintain the interest and, where possible, the involvement of executives in specific parts of your program, such as community services that contribute to the stability of the neighborhood or educational programs that might benefit employees.
3. Invite local executives to visit your organization and see your programs in action, on a nonobligatory basis.
4. Show evidence of good management, such as a balanced budget and well-conceived long-range plans.
5. If you haven't already done so, begin reporting to past corporate donors on what their support has meant in enabling your organization to expand and/or strengthen its programs, to construct new programs to meet new problems, or (in the case of restricted grants) to further develop the projects for which the grants were made.
6. Be sure to acknowledge corporate support in ways that are commensurate with the size and scope of the contributions. This subject is covered in the chapter on acknowledgments of contributions.
7. Keep local executives informed of budgeted items in those programs that might be of significant relevance to their companies, such as salary support of faculty or staff who are involved in corporation-related teaching, training programs, market or industrial research, special equipment, and special programs.
8. Place executives on your mailing list for annual reports, newsletters, and other appropriate publications.
9. Make sure your publications reflect the quality and worth of your programs and how they contribute to society as a whole. Stress these points in every presentation or proposal for corporate support.
10. Do not take corporate support for granted. Acknowledgment of past support should be a major part of every proposal for a new contribution.

Make every effort to retain the interest of past corporate donors in all of the ways previously suggested, and any others that you can think of or devise.

PREPARING THE PROPOSAL

The preparation of a proposal for a corporate contribution should be preceded by a preliminary contact made by telephone, by letter, or by a personal visit to learn whether the proposal matches the company's objectives or interests. An inquiry should be made, also, about the way in which the proposal should be presented. Some companies prefer a brief cover letter, while others require a completed questionnaire or formal application document. Still others request a brief pre-proposal letter summarizing the basic elements of the project for which support is being requested, together with a budget and some background information about the structure and objectives of your organization.

Supporting Documents

Prior to attaching supporting documents which you feel may strengthen your case, seek instructions from the company regarding the specific information that is required, and send only that.

The Proposal

The specific content of proposals necessarily varies, but corporate funders regard the following information as basic:

1. Unless otherwise directed, the proposal letter itself should not exceed two pages. Additional required information should be assembled as attachments.
2. A clear statement, in the first paragraph, should indicate exactly what you are seeking support for and the cost of the project.

3. Background information about your organization should include its past accomplishments, new developments, present programs, and program objectives, as well as your programmatic capital and endowment goals.
4. The proposal should state the need for the project being proposed, the plan of action, an operational timetable, a breakdown of costs, and the relationship between the proposed project and the overall programs and objectives of the asking organization.
5. A copy of the annual budget should be attached.

In the highly competitive quest for corporate gifts, staff development officers often can provide missing links in proposals by intensively researching each prospect. Readily available literature will describe the company's products, services, interests, and areas of concern geographically and by subject area.

Timing of Your Proposal

Many companies have specific deadlines for the submission of proposals within a fiscal year. Others have more flexible policies regarding the receipt of proposals. It is essential to identify all existing deadlines observed by your corporate prospects, and carefully time your proposals accordingly.

PRESENTATION

The importance of personal contact in seeking any major gift has been stated and restated many times. The selection of the person or persons to make the contact is especially important. Business executives generally are on the same "wave length," and the corporate prospect is more likely to respond favorably to an appeal being made by another corporate executive, especially one who is at least equal in stature. The presence of the president as a resource person can be of great help in the discussion.

It often helps if the prospect can be induced to make a site visit to your organization, where he or she can meet some of the individuals who will be involved in the project being proposed as well as other major players, such as your president, board members, staff members, and anyone who might add another dimension to the discussion.

The development officer also should make sure that the volunteers, who will be calling on your prospects, are well informed about your organization's history, objectives, financial condition, specific needs, and any features of your program that are unique. They also should be well informed about the company's officers, board members, present economic conditions, grant limitations, priorities, and interests.

FOLLOW-THROUGH

After all of the negotiations have been completed and a grant is received, appropriate acknowledgment and recognition should follow shortly thereafter. Remember that proper acknowledgment of a grant is the first step in cultivating the donor's continued interest and support.

Acknowledging Rejections

If your proposal is rejected, write a letter thanking the corporation or corporate foundation for taking the time to consider and process your proposal. Frequently the reason for rejection is insufficient funds. This situation easily could change by the following year, and a courteous thank you may give your next proposal a better chance of being accepted.

What You Can Do Tomorrow: Soliciting Corporations

1. Secure and analyze the membership directory of your local chamber of commerce and/or other logical sources to make sure that your corporate prospect list is complete.
2. Prepare a preproposal mailing to each corporation on your list, addressed to its chief executive officer, inquiring

whether your programs match their interests, and requesting instructions regarding (as in the case of foundations) the submission of proposals or grant applications.

3. Prepare a list of recommended candidates for the chairperson of your corporate committee, for presentation to your general campaign chairperson (in the event that the appointment has not yet been made).

SOLICITING FOUNDATIONS

*F*oundations represent an enormously rich funding source for grants ranging from moderate to massive. The potential of foundation giving warrants whatever expenditure of time and effort is necessary to properly research, cultivate, explore, and, finally, identify those foundations whose interests match yours, and then make your contacts in the prescribed manner.

A foundation may be defined as a nongovernmental, non-profit organization having a principal fund of its own, managed by its own trustees or directors, and established to maintain or aid social, educational, charitable, religious, or other activities serving the common welfare.

PREPARATION

An effective foundation giving program actually is carried on in two stages—one at the staff level, and the other at the volunteer level.

At the Staff Level

Careful research of directories and other sources of information is required to produce the following:

1. A list of foundations (prospects), local and elsewhere, whose stated purposes and objectives match those of your organization.

2. Published guidelines or stated preferences for each foundation regarding the manner of approach. If this information is not available in directories, write or call the foundation office.
3. Lists of programs or projects that mesh with the interests of the foundations.
4. Identification of suitable candidates for chairperson of the campaign's foundation committee.

At the Volunteer Level

1. The general campaign chairperson should appoint a chairperson of the foundation committee.
2. The chairperson of the foundation committee should, in turn, recruit a sufficient number of workers to contact all of the foundations to be covered, on an assignment basis of not more than five foundations per solicitor.
3. During the recruiting process, it is essential that all volunteers receive written descriptions of their respective responsibilities, including required attendance at an orientation meeting.

ORIENTATION

Orientation meetings should be chaired by the committee chairperson and should include the following agenda items:

1. Greetings and introduction of those present
2. Description of the programs and objectives of the organization (by the chief executive officer or other qualified staff executive)
3. Explanation of the campaign plan (by the chairperson and staff campaign director or other qualified staff member)
4. Distribution of campaign materials and explanation regarding their use (by campaign staff executive)
5. Assignment of or selection of prospects (this may require a separate meeting or may stand as the last item in the agenda, depending on the length of the orientation session)
6. Questions and answers

PLAN OF ACTION

1. Contact each foundation in the manner prescribed by its published or stated guidelines.
2. Follow through with appropriate visits to and by foundation officials. Site visits should be encouraged wherever possible, so that these grantmakers can see your programs in action. Often, more than one meeting is required before your proposal is accepted or rejected.
3. Provide appropriate expressions of appreciation for grants that are received, commensurate with the sizes and natures of the contributions.
4. Thank the foundation for taking the time to consider your proposal, in the event that it is rejected.
5. Properly acknowledge the efforts, services, and achievements of everyone who was involved in the foundation solicitation program.

FOUNDATION RESEARCH

In order to solicit foundations effectively, development officers and volunteers must understand the characteristics of the different types of foundations and the procedures that should be followed in the preparation and submission of proposals that stand the best chance of being funded.

There are a number of excellent directories that contain this kind of information, but the one that is recommended by most foundation executives and development officers is *The Foundation Directory*, published by The Foundation Center in New York City. The *Directory* is designed to serve as a primary resource for the development and classification of foundation prospect lists, and has a wealth of general information covering just about every aspect of foundation giving. The *Directory* provides information on the finances, operations, and giving interests of the nation's largest grantmaking foundations— those with assets of $1 million or more or which have annual giving of at least $100,000.

The chart on pages 90–91, reproduced from the *Directory*, summarizes the general characteristics of the four major

General Characteristics of Four Types of Foundations

Foundation Type	Description	Source of Funds	Decision-making Body	Grantmaking Activity	Reporting Requirements
Independent foundation	An independent grantmaking organization established to aid social, educational, religious, or other charitable activities	Endowment generally derived from a single source such as an individual, a family, or a group of individuals. Contributions to endowment limited as to tax deductibility	Decisions may be made by donor or members of donor's family; by an independent board of directors or trustees; or by a bank or trust officer acting on donor's behalf	Broad discretionary giving allowed but may have specific guidelines and give only in a few specific fields. About 70% limit their giving to local area	Annual information returns 990-PF filed with IRS must be made available to public. A small percentage issue separately printed annual reports
Company-sponsored foundation	Legally an independent grantmaking organization with close ties to the corporation providing funds	Endowment and annual contributions from a profit-making corporation. May maintain small endowment and pay out most of contributions received annually in grants, or may maintain endowment to cover contributions in years when corporate profits are down	Decisions made by board of directors often composed of corporate officials, but which may include individuals with no corporate affiliation. Decisions may also be made by local company officials	Giving tends to be in fields related to corporate activities or in communities where corporation operates. Usually give more grants but in smaller dollar amounts than independent foundations	Same as above

(continued)

General Characteristics of Four Types of Foundations (continued)

Foundation Type	Description	Source of Funds	Decision-making Body	Grantmaking Activity	Reporting Requirements
Operating foundation	An organization which uses its resources to conduct research or provide a direct service	Endowment usually provided from a single source, but eligible for maximum tax deductible contributions from public	Decisions generally made by independent board of directors	Makes few, if any, grants. Grants generally related directly to the foundation's program	Same as above
Community foundation	A publicly-supported organization which makes grants for social, educational, religious, or other charitable purposes in a specific community or region	Contributions received from many donors. Usually eligible for maximum tax deductible contributions from public	Decisions made by board of directors representing the diversity of the community	Grants generally limited to charitable organizations in local community	IRS 990 return available to public. Many publish full guidelines or annual reports

Source: The Foundation Directory, The Foundation Center, 11th Edition, 1987.

categories or types of foundations. The information contained in this chart provides a broad base of knowledge for a better understanding of the nature of foundations, which you might want to circulate among your volunteers and members of your staff.

Practical Advice from Foundation Executives

In preparation for this chapter, I reviewed many guidelines, articles, and speeches by foundation grantmakers for specific recommendations that would assist seekers of foundation funding. The following material is from speeches made by foundation executives Mr. William N. Clark, Mrs. Marion M. Faldet, and Dr. Manning M. Patillo, who represent a good cross-section of foundation giving.

All three emphasized that grant seekers need to identify and contact only those foundations whose interests and objectives matched theirs. Further, grant seekers should make their initial approaches in accordance with the published guidelines or otherwise stated preferences of the foundations they are planning to contact. In doing so, they should send foundations only the information and materials requested.

Two also recommended The Foundation Directory as a principal resource for foundations research. They emphasized the desirability of making an initial contact through an informal letter outlining the nature of your project and asking whether the foundation would be interested in receiving a full proposal or a formal application. They advised against dropping in without an appointment.

In addition, their summarized specific recommendations follow.

Mr. William N. Clark, former executive director, The Robert R. McCormick Charitable Trust, former chairman of the board, The Donors' Forum of Chicago:

Preparation. Do not plan to ask for money for a project or a purpose that is inconsistent with your mission just because it appears to be more consistent with the foundation's interests.

The Proposal. There is no magic formula for a good proposal. Its objective is to convey the fact that you need money for a specific purpose, plus an explanation of why you need it. Common sense, clarity, and brevity, consistent with completeness, apply.

The proposal should begin with a statement requesting a grant for a specific amount needed to fund all or a designated portion of an appropriate project. Virtually all foundations require a copy of your most recent annual audit or comparable annual financial statement in addition to budgets for the coming year or for the project being proposed.

Initial Contact. Do not do the following:

- Insist on delivering the proposal in person.
- Submit proposals in thick binders with oversize paper and an overabundance of supporting material.
- Call the foundation executive to ask if he or she has any questions.
- Use too many words and/or offensive jargon.
- "Doll up" the proposal in leather binding with silver braid and gold lettering. This is just window dressing and will not impress an experienced foundation official. Too much attention to appearances may seem to reflect bad taste or a preoccupation with trivialities.

Accountability. Most foundations will ask the recipient of a grant to submit a report within a specified time, accounting for the use of the funds. The grantee should submit a report whether or not the foundation asks for it. If circumstances arise that make it impossible or undesirable to use the funds for the originally intended purpose, the foundation should be informed immediately, so that it may permit the funds to be used for another purpose, or request that the funds be returned. Finally, don't ever hesitate to ask a foundation executive for advice and assistance when you feel that you really need it.

Mrs. Marion M. Faldet, vice president and secretary, The Spencer Foundation:

Your success is bringing outside funding back to your institution. Our success is finding the right projects to support. It is important for development officers and foundation officials to work together and to have compatible relationships [in speaking to development directors].

Development practices which "turn off" a foundation official:

1. Failing to discern the foundations' interests
2. Dropping in without an appointment
3. Bringing a "shopping list" of projects
4. Bringing a proposal for preliminary review "on the spot"
5. Sending batches of material for the foundation "to keep on file"

Practices that "turn on" foundation officials:

1. Calling or writing to inquire by mail or appointment the ways in which your needs and the foundations' needs can mesh
2. Following application procedures
3. Filing a credible proposal
4. Accepting the foundation board's decision graciously

Dr. Manning M. Patillo, former president of The Foundation Center, former president, The Danforth Foundation, and president emeritus, Oglethorpe University:

Soundly administered foundations must separate the carefully conceived, workable proposals from the superficial, poorly planned, or inconsequential ones. The applicant should operate on the assumption that he is dealing with people of good judgment who know what they are doing.

Preliminary Steps Prior to Submission of Proposals. Submit proposals one at a time rather than simultaneously. Often a request is sent to eight or ten foundations at the same time with the hope that one of them may show interest. This kind of mass solicitation is expensive in foundation staff time and occasionally leads to embarrassment. When a proposal submitted by a respected university to two foundations simultaneously resulted in two grants, the administration was in the awkward position of having to apologize and decline one of the grants.

Follow-ups. Once a request is submitted to a foundation, the initiative usually lies with the prospective donor. Every foundation has its own procedure for initial consideration of applications, and the determination of what further steps should be taken to evaluate the proposal.

What to Do If Your Project Is Turned Down. Most foundations face the unhappy necessity of declining many sound requests simply because the funds are not currently available to support all the good proposals.

If your request is turned down by a foundation, thank them for taking the time to process your proposal, and then look for another appropriate foundation. An applicant with a promising proposal and persistence can almost always secure the funds required sooner or later.

Essential Ingredients

1. Have an idea and a clearly thought-out plan of action for achievement.
2. Describe your project or program in straightforward English with a minimum of technical jargon.
3. Include a statement of purpose, why it is important, how it is to be achieved, what specific results might be expected, who will direct the work, how much it will cost, and why your organization is the proper one to undertake this project.
4. The proposal should have a covering letter from the president or other appropriate officer providing assurance that the project has the official backing of the organization.

HOW FOUNDATIONS EVALUATE REQUESTS

Each foundation maintains its own guidelines for evaluating grant requests. These criteria may vary sharply between one foundation and another. Most foundation executives probably consider, somewhere in their deliberations, these six factors, listed in their probable sequence:

1. Does the project match our interests?
2. Does the project fit into our budget?
3. Does the project duplicate programs or services already being provided by another agency?
4. Does the project promise results that would be important enough to warrant an investment by the foundation?
5. Does the project appear feasible on the basis of the quality of the organization's leadership and other resources?
6. Does the project have sufficient appeal (in the view of the foundation executive doing the initial appraisal) to win the approval of my staff, colleagues, and the governing board?

Note: A person of stature who proposes a project with which he or she demonstrates true familiarity can be an important factor in securing a favorable evaluation.

COMMENTS

No single group of prospects is more abused than are foundations. The most common reason for this abuse by development offices is lack of knowledge about the foundation's interests. Printed guidelines and otherwise stated preferences of most foundations corroborate the views of our three friends; and further substantiate the observations of many development "scholars" regarding the absence of any major changes in basic fund-raising characteristics.

What You Can Do Tomorrow: Soliciting Foundations

1. Begin a study of *The Foundation Directory* or other appropriate directories to identify every foundation with program interests that match yours.
2. Prepare brief letters to each of these foundations, summarizing the project for which you are seeking support and asking for instructions regarding the submission of proposals or grant applications.
3. Prepare a list of recommended candidates for the chairperson of your foundation committee for presentation to your general campaign chairperson (in the event that the appointment has not yet been made).

SOLICITING ORGANIZED GROUPS

 M any organized groups provide enthusiastic and generous support to campaigns conducted by nonprofit organizations with whom they have mutual program interests. This support generally is in the form of treasury gifts, which sometimes are supplemented by individual contributions from members.

The objectives of an organized groups campaign should be to reach every organized social, fraternal, service, veterans, woman's, youth, farm, labor, and church group in your community. In addition to being an important potential funding source, organized groups provide a valuable outlet for your educational materials and general information about your organization and its programs.

There are a number of ways in which your organized groups campaign can be planned and implemented. The following steps, in the sequence indicated, should be considered for incorporation in any plan:

1. Have your general campaign chairperson appoint a chairperson for your organized groups division.
2. Prepare a comprehensive list of all of the clubs and organizations in your area by classification, including service clubs, social, veterans, and church groups. In each case, identify the club president or secretary, total membership, dates and places of regular meetings, previous giving experience, known areas of interest, and any other information that the solicitor might find helpful.

3. Determine and recruit the number of volunteers needed to head each group classification, using your year-round volunteers as leadership sources, whenever possible.
4. Have your group chairpersons enlist their respective teams of workers, on the basis of one for every three organizations to be contacted.
5. Plan meetings of group chairpersons for purposes of describing strategic ways of making the campaign a success from the following standpoints:
   - contributions
   - opportunities for public education
   - opportunities to cultivate the interests of club members in becoming volunteers in your organization's regular programs.

6. Plan briefing sessions for all workers to be sure that they understand your campaign plan, to provide them with literature and other materials, and to be sure that they are conversant with the history, programs, and needs of your organization.
7. (Group chairpersons) Secure endorsements from each club in your group and request permission, well in advance, for your workers to present appeals to members at a regular meeting, using films, if available, and/or other appropriate visuals. These appearances should be scheduled for a time when all of the other campaign divisions have completed their solicitations.
8. (Workers) When you make your presentation, remember to request a treasury gift and/or earmarked contribution from members, to take an opportunity to distribute your educational literature, and to secure the names of members who would be interested in becoming volunteers in your organization.

ACKNOWLEDGMENTS

Sincere and well-constructed acknowledgments of support received from organized groups are especially important for a variety of reasons:

1. This is the first step in cultivating their continued support.
2. Organized groups who support your program may prove to be a rich source of volunteers to work in future campaigns.
3. Organized groups are an excellent potential resource in helping your organization to keep its programs and objectives before the public.

In addition to letters of thanks from combinations of your high level leadership, consider presenting inexpensive certificates of appreciation to club officers at your annual—or at a special—meeting. When particular clubs raise unusually large sums of money, you might choose to invite their officers to make formal check presentations at your meeting. Appropriate publicity should be planned jointly by officers of the contributing clubs and of benefiting organizations.

COMMENT

After the organized groups campaign has been completed, hold meetings with officials of contributing clubs to explore possible areas of mutual interest, with a view toward securing consideration of related projects or programs for their continued support, with appropriate name recognition.

RESIDENTIAL SOLICITATION

*T*he objectives of a residential campaign are to reach every family in selected communities to obtain a thoughtful contribution and to leave educational literature of interest or use to the family unit.

One of the more successful residential campaigns in the United States is conducted by the American Cancer Society each April. The stated objectives of the Residential Crusade are to provide every family with life-saving information about cancer and to secure a thoughtful contribution. The educational component of such a campaign clearly emphasizes to the volunteer the importance of making personal calls to every household in an assigned area. As State Campaign Director of the ACS Illinois Division for 12 years, it was obvious to me and to my colleagues that this sense of mission on the part of volunteer Crusaders played a major role in the steady increase in the amount of dollars raised, as well as in the number of dedicated volunteers who joined the ranks of the Crusaders.

Other organizations have incorporated educational or service components into their residential campaigns, and the results have been rewarding.

The structures of residential campaigns necessarily differ from one another, but there are some basic guidelines that should be considered by every organization that is involved in residential campaigning:

1. *Early planning and careful timing are essential.* To build up and retain the interest of a large volunteer organization requires precise timing and careful planning. If volunteers are

enlisted too early, they may forget or lose interest and drop out before the solicitation period begins. If they are enlisted at the last minute, they may not receive adequate instructions in time, may misunderstand these instructions, or may not receive their materials in time. Overextended periods of solicitation cause many volunteers to lose interest. The residential campaign period should be limited to a reasonable time frame, and the volunteer's assignment should be limited to a reasonable and easily manageable number. With adequate publicity, careful planning, and adequate coverage, many one-night campaigns have proven quite successful.

2. *The objectives of the residential campaign should be clearly identified.*
3. *The specific assignments and responsibilities of all concerned should be clearly stated in writing and discussed during the process of recruitment.*
4. *The city, suburb, or community must be divided into manageable units.* In order to do this efficiently, the following may be helpful:
   A. Obtain large, clear maps of the city and its suburbs. Sources for such maps include city or county planning commissions, chambers of commerce, post office districts, city engineers, housing development or suburban real estate firms, and oil companies.
   B. Secure reverse telephone directories where available (listings by street and number).
   C. Check with city directories, precinct lists, or other directories showing street divisions.

Advice and assistance often can be secured from city planning departments, chambers of commerce, election committees, and area development departments of large corporations, especially utilities.

DIVISION OF AREAS

In planning the division of areas, organize each neighborhood unit and each suburb separately. Divide large population areas into subdivisions of approximately 25,000 to 30,000 people. Outline each suburb and each unit on street maps, and assign each its own chairperson.

The subdivisions indicated above should be further broken down into units of 150 to 200 residences, using school districts and political precincts as guides. Each of these smaller districts should be outlined on maps and assigned to a captain.

In making the final breakdown into units for assignment to residential solicitors, you must first decide how many residences each will be expected to cover. The largest assignment should be 25 residences, but the effectiveness of solicitors seems to increase as this number is lowered to approach 10.

In an area where only the population figure is available, the number of households can be estimated by dividing the population figure by 3.2, which is the estimated national average of individuals in a household. The number of volunteers needed to cover an area can be easily estimated by dividing the number of residences to be assigned to each solicitor into the number of homes in that area. Reliable estimates of the population, or the number of homes in a particular area can be obtained from one or more of the following sources:

- Local chamber of commerce, public or newspaper library
- County clerk, tax or county planning commissioner
- Latest United States Census Bureau report
- Public utility companies

DISTRICT CHAIRPERSONS, CAPTAINS, AND SOLICITORS

There are many sources of volunteers for residential campaigns conducted by local organizations that carry on local programs. Listed below are some of these sources which have proven to be exceptionally productive:

- Officers and members of woman's clubs and organizations, service clubs, religious groups, PTAs, auxiliaries of fraternal and veterans' groups, and other local organizations

- Past donors of major gifts
- Past and present officers, governing board members, and other volunteers
- Persons who have been served by your organization
- Friends and neighbors recruited by your volunteers

Using the pyramid method of building the necessary forces of volunteers, the recommended categories of leadership and the responsibilities of each are outlined as follows:

District Chairpersons

1. The general residential chairperson should recruit a district chairperson for each area of approximately 25,000 residents.
2. Residential chairpersons should have no other duties.
3. The district chairperson's primary duty is to enlist a captain for each area of approximately 150 to 200 residences within the district.
4. The residential chairperson and district chairperson should be enlisted early—at least four months before solicitation begins.
5. The district chairperson should plan to hold orientation meetings for captains and solicitors to inform them about the organization's programs and campaign procedures.

Captains

1. Captains should be responsible for enrolling sufficient numbers of solicitors to cover neighborhoods of approximately 150 to 200 residences.
2. Captains are responsible for the collection of funds raised by the solicitors, preferably during the late evening after the calls have been made. In this connection, collection stations should be set up in centrally located places, where the solicitors can bring their returns.

3. Captains who experience difficulty in enrolling sufficient numbers of solicitors should contact their district chairpersons for assistance.

VOLUNTEER SOLICITORS

There are two ways in which a volunteer force of solicitors can be developed in adequate numbers to cover designated areas. One is through the traditional chain of command, where the captains do all of the recruiting. This is preferable because these solicitors can provide the base for future campaign organizations.

The second method is to ask the memberships of existing organizations within the community to solicit as a club project or on an individual basis. This method, however, does not help to build a permanent residential campaign organization, but it may be the best method available in some communities and should not be overlooked.

Materials

The following materials should be supplied to each volunteer solicitor for use in his or her approach:

1. Campaign "kit" envelopes large enough to hold all solicitation materials, to be returned to campaign headquarters at the completion of the campaign.
2. Volunteer solicitor identification badges which identify the volunteer and the organization.
3. Mass distribution educational leaflets (as many as are needed to cover the residences assigned to the solicitor), which explain the organization, its goals, its specific campaign mission, and the message that you wish to convey.
4. Report forms on which donors' names, addresses, and amounts can be recorded.
5. Self-addressed "Sorry I missed you" envelopes which are to be left at residences where volunteers cannot make

personal contact. Generally, four of these envelopes should be included in the kit for every 15 residences assigned to the solicitor.

6. Solicitor instruction sheets, which detail the dates and times of the campaign, the specific areas assigned to the volunteer, any information the volunteer needs to complete the solicitation, and instructions for returning the money collected to the headquarters.

OFFICE PROCEDURES AND RECORDS

The primary purpose for complying with required office procedures and record keeping is to ensure that all matters relating to the servicing of the vast army of volunteers are handled quickly and accurately. Office routine should provide for files to be kept up to date and easily accessible.

Reporting Enlistment of Volunteers

Captains should submit to campaign headquarters the name, address, telephone number, the area number (ward and precinct), and the assignments for each volunteer enlisted.

Acknowledgments and Reminders

Immediately after enlistment, the volunteer solicitor should receive an appropriate acknowledgment postcard or letter from campaign headquarters. A reminder card or note should be sent about ten days before the campaign.

PREPARATION

Here are five points to consider before the solicitation period begins:

1. Do all chairpersons and captains have accurate listings of all volunteers, so that they may be invited to meetings for a review of final plans?

2. During the week prior to the residential campaign, has each captain been given a list of his or her volunteer solicitors (names, addresses, telephone numbers) as well as each solicitor's specific collection area? One copy of this should be given to the captain, one copy to the chairperson, and one copy retained in the permanent files at campaign headquarters.
3. Has a speedy and efficient system for the counting and banking of money been set up?
4. Have you arranged for trained staff or volunteers to handle telephone inquiries in campaign headquarters immediately prior to and during the solicitation period?
5. Have your volunteer solicitors received (by mail or delivery by their captains) their solicitation material kits several days before the residential campaign? The reason for delivering or mailing this material just before the campaign is to make sure that it will not be mislaid or used before the actual campaign date. Also, receiving this material the week before the campaign reminds the volunteer of his or her commitment to serve.

SOLICITATION

If no one is at home when the volunteer calls, he or she should make a return visit or leave a self-mailing envelope (provided in the kit), together with one of the mass distribution educational leaflets. A reasonably high percentage of people mail these envelopes back within the next several days.

Volunteer solicitors should be reminded not to contact residences that are not assigned to them. To do so may confuse those assigned to make the calls, and the families who are contacted more than one time.

After the solicitor has covered the assigned territory, he or she should return the kit (with contributions) to a predesignated place or to the captain, according to the arrangements made for this purpose. Since assignments are made on a geographic basis, advance "appointment-making" telephone calls are highly impractical if not impossible.

Police Protection

Arrangements should be made to provide police protection wherever considerable sums of money are accumulated, handled, or transported. Police should be on duty at the central collection points for one-night campaigns from the time the money starts coming in until it has been counted and banked.

BANKING PROCEDURE

It is essential that a sound banking procedure be set up. Ask the bank handling your organization's account to help count and deposit the money raised as a public service. Banks also offer many valuable suggestions. Below are a few which may prove helpful.

Counting the Money

Where possible, have the money counted by bank tellers. They are trained to do this faster and with greater accuracy. If tellers are not available, use regular volunteers or staff. In order to provide early reports of progress, money should be counted as rapidly as possible.

The following procedure for counting and processing contributions is recommended:

1. Each report envelope should be opened, and its contents noted on the outside of the envelope by the captain. All captains' returns are consolidated by districts. The captain reports totals to the district chairperson.
2. Each envelope should be checked carefully a second time, preferably by a second person to ensure that money is not inadvertently overlooked.
3. At the bank, the tellers' count should be recorded by district, for reporting purposes.
4. Money should be banked as soon as possible.
5. All envelopes and all other material in the kits should be saved and transmitted to campaign headquarters.

RURAL SOLICITATION

All of the suggestions which apply to residential campaigns in cities and towns can be adapted to rural areas. In general, rural residential chairpersons have responsibility for the campaign in all territories not covered by city or suburban residential chairpersons:

- They appoint chairpersons for each township.
- They promote attendance at training meetings.
- They give support, where necessary, in recruiting solicitors.
- They oversee the township chairperson's responsibilities for delivery of solicitors' kits and collection and deposit of contributions in designated banks.

Rural chairpersons should enlist solicitors in sufficient number to cover each road or section of a road in each township. In some rural communities, coverage is achieved by using school bus routes or mail delivery routes.

APARTMENT HOUSE SOLICITATION

"Apartment house" here includes rooming houses, individual large buildings, series of large buildings (such as multiunit housing), garden apartments, and trailer courts.

An apartment house committee should be organized to plan the best type of coverage for large buildings. Its role is to enlist a captain for each building, who in turn would secure solicitors for each ten or fifteen apartments. Where there are fewer than ten apartments in a building, one person per building should be sufficient.

In the cases of large garden apartment buildings containing four to six units, captains should be enrolled with the responsibility of enlisting one solicitor for each set of two buildings.

A central apartment house committee should be set up, with one person for each district having the responsibility for covering the numerous apartment houses within its borders.

The following procedures for solicitation should be considered where appropriate:

1. The best results generally are realized when one individual is assigned the responsibility for organizing solicitation of an apartment house.
2. Where management refuses door-to-door solicitation, ask for permission to have a volunteer place a leaflet and return mailing envelope under each door, addressed back to the volunteer or to campaign headquarters.
3. As a final resort, send appeal letters to individual apartment residents.

ADDITIONAL COMMENTS

Door-to-door solicitation of residences should be restricted to adult volunteers. If children are used, they should be accompanied by adults in every case.

There are many participants in a residential crusade: volunteers, contributors, public and private officials (who issue proclamations, provide protection, grant approvals and endorsements), media officials, bank officials, and numerous others. It is essential to acknowledge their efforts, commensurate with the size and nature of their "contributions." Remember that appropriate expressions of appreciation comprise the first step in planning and organizing next year's campaign.

Acknowledgment Postcard

Every American Cancer Society volunteer solicitor should receive an acknowledgment postcard from headquarters within 48 hours of acceptance. A sample card should have ample space for the insertion of the typed label outlining the territory to be visited. (*Note:* The other side of postcard for address only.)

PLEASE SAVE THIS CARD! This Is Your OFFICIAL Identification!

Many thanks for your willingness to help in the relentless war against CANCER in this year's CAMPAIGN. The territory you will cover is:

> **9 thru 43 Salisbury Rd.**
>
> **AS7-8195**

You will receive your Volunteer Worker's Kit by ___(Date)___

REMEMBER	**American Cancer Society, Inc.**
Print Date and Time in	Unit address and phone
this space	number of Headquarters

Source: American Cancer Society Guidebook for Residential Solicitation.

Sample County Residential Organizational Chart

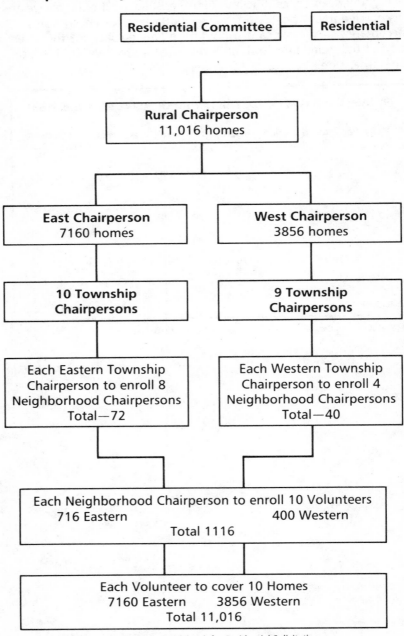

Source: American Cancer Society Guidebook for Residential Solicitation.

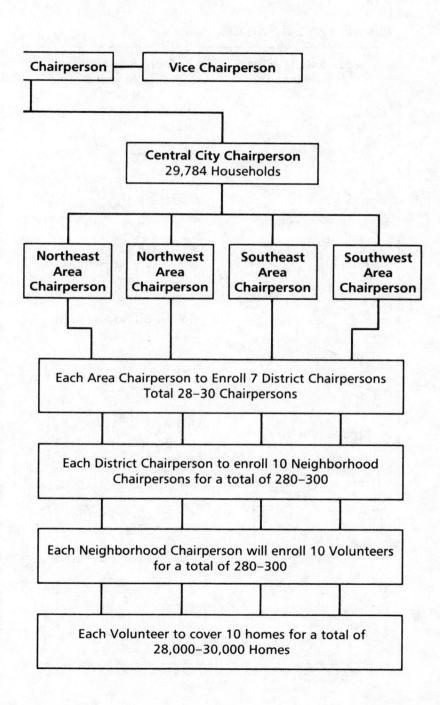

Plan for Subdividing City Map

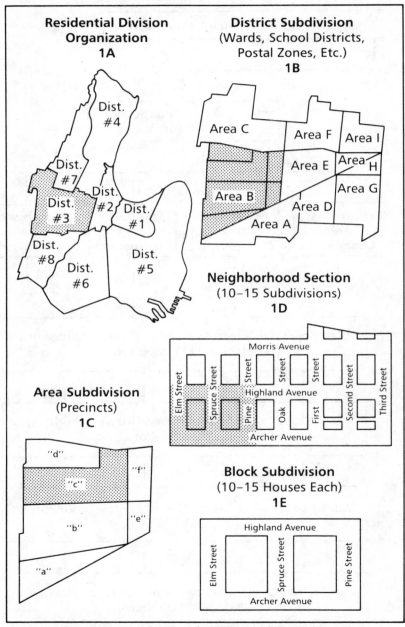

Residential Division Organization 1A

District Subdivision (Wards, School Districts, Postal Zones, Etc.) 1B

Dist. #4, Dist. #7, Dist. #2, Dist. #3, Dist. #1, Dist. #8, Dist. #6, Dist. #5

Area C, Area F, Area I, Area E, Area H, Area B, Area G, Area D, Area A

Neighborhood Section (10–15 Subdivisions) 1D

Morris Avenue, Highland Avenue, Archer Avenue
Elm Street, Spruce Street, Pine Street, Oak, First, Second Street, Third Street

Area Subdivision (Precincts) 1C

"d", "f", "c", "e", "b", "a"

Block Subdivision (10–15 Houses Each) 1E

Highland Avenue, Archer Avenue
Elm Street, Spruce Street, Pine Street

Source: American Cancer Society Guidebook for Residential Solicitation.

Suggested Control Chart for Units in Residential Solicitation

District	Quota	Raised	Population	# Families	Volunteers			Captains			Rosters		Kits			Training meetings			Chairperson
					Needed	Enrolled	Worked	Needed	Enrolled	Worked	Made	Delivered	Labelled	Mailed	Delivered	Planned	Date held	Attendance	

Districts, Wards, Precincts, etc., can be listed alphabetically or numerically.
Additional columns may be used to indicate other areas of interest to the particular Unit.
Examples:
   Pyramid organization or telephone recruitment
   Per capita income for 19____
   Per household income for 19____
   Per capita ACS income
American Cancer Society Guidebook for Residential Solicitation.

Sample of Analysis Sheet for Use in Residential Soliciting

Districts	Total # Volunteers Who Worked	Total # Volunteers Needed	# not assigned*	# kits returned containing money	# kits not returned	# kits not worked	# units of residences not worked*	Total income from kits	Average per kit	Total "not at home" envelopes with money**	Average per envelope	Total from residential campaign	Total # of $5.00 contributions	Total # of $10.00 contributions	Total # $25.00 or more contributions	Total # $5.00 or more new contributions	Total # $5.00 or more contributions repeating*	Total # $5.00 or more contributions not repeating	Total # orientation meetings	Attendance at orientation meetings	Were rosters used?

*Refers to the Units of Residences (ten or fifteen homes per assignment).
**Refers to those repeating their contributions for two or more years.
Other columns may be added to suit the unit.
American Cancer Society Guidebook for Residential Solicitation.

Independent Business Solicitation

*I*ndependent business is an extremely important and often overlooked source of income and should be considered for inclusion in virtually every fund-raising operation. Local organizations engaged in health, welfare, social, civic, educational, and cultural programs generally are regarded as "anchors" which contribute to the stability of the neighborhood and make it a better place in which to live and do business. Accordingly, the business community traditionally is responsive to requests for their support.

The independent business division of your organization should be headed by a chairperson appointed by the general campaign chairperson. The objective of this division should be to reach every person who owns, manages, operates, or works in an independent business, to request contributions from the establishment and from the individuals who work there. This should be done by personal calls.

The field of operation should include every store, shop, market, restaurant, studio, professional office, and other commercial establishment located in shopping centers, office buildings, arcades, and business areas of every community that are not contacted by any other division of the campaign.

A logical first step in organizing for independent business solicitation is to assemble prospect lists from one or a combination of the following sources:

- Telephone company street directories
- Chambers of commerce lists
- Local business directories

- Business people with knowledge of the areas
- Shopping center or arcade directories

OFFICE BUILDINGS

Multistory office buildings require special handling because business directories do not indicate floor locations of offices and shops, only street addresses. For this reason, visits must be made to building lobbies where floor directories can be copied and transmitted to prospect lists.

ENDORSEMENTS, PERMISSIONS, AND AGREEMENTS OF COOPERATION

In most business campaigns, permission to solicit must be obtained from local municipalities, chambers of commerce, or other business associations. It should be the responsibility of the independent business chairperson to obtain these clearances, and, where possible, endorsements and agreements of cooperation.

ORGANIZATION

There are a number of ways in which business areas can be organized for solicitation. The following examples may help you to choose or design the method that best fits your situation:

1. Recruit an area or team captain for each ten-block area. The area captain in turn should recruit one worker for each block.
2. Recruit a team captain for each office building, who should, in turn, recruit one worker for each floor.
3. Recruit a team captain for each arcade, who should, in turn, recruit one worker for each ten shops.
4. Recruit a team captain for each shopping center, who should, in turn, recruit one worker for each ten shops.

Note: Team chairpersons and workers respectively should be oriented during the recruitment process, and given written instructions outlining their specific responsibilities.

Area maps must be secured, marked off, and copies given to appropriate team captains for their use in worker recruitment and orientation. These maps should be checked and referenced with other campaign divisions to avoid duplicate solicitation.

TIMING

Independent business solicitation should be conducted at the beginning of the campaign, preferably within a two- or three-day period during the middle of the week.

CAMPAIGN MATERIALS

Each campaign worker should receive the following:

- An instruction sheet
- A prospect list
- A contribution card for each prospect (with detachable receipt stubs)
- Contributor cards for new businesses and offices
- A piece of educational literature for each prospect.

Note: The use of contribution cards provides an important psychological dimension which elevates the solicitation from the status of a collection to that of a regular campaign operation.

Materials may be given to the solicitors at the time of recruitment or at a subsequent orientation meeting. Every volunteer at every level should receive written instructions, outlining specific responsibilities, and directions regarding the receipting, reporting, and handling of contributions.

MEETINGS

It is recommended that a kickoff meeting—breakfast or luncheon—be considered in addition to individual orientation at time of recruitment. At that meeting, kits can be distributed to workers who do not have them, and answers given to any last-minute questions that anyone may have regarding the campaign in general or their specific assignments in particular. A report meeting also should be held immediately after the close of the solicitation period to determine progress and necessary clean-up activities.

ACKNOWLEDGMENTS

As in the case of every other phase of the general campaign, letters and other appropriate expressions of appreciation should be sent to all of the volunteers and others who endorsed, assisted, or supported the independent business solicitation in any way.

FORMS

The exact types of necessary forms may vary from one area to another, but the following samples offer practical suggestions.

Captain's Acknowledgment Letter

Date

Name
Address
City, State

Dear _____:

I am writing to express again my deep appreciation for your agreement to serve as a business captain in our campaign to support the important work of the [insert the name of your organization].

Enclosed is a copy of our latest annual report, which I hope you will find interesting and useful in answering questions. Also enclosed are duplicate copies of prospects' lists for each of the campaign assignments for the workers that you will be recruiting. As soon as you have completed your recruitment of solicitors, please fill in their names, business addresses, and phone numbers, and return the lists to campaign headquarters.

After the information has been recorded, the lists will be returned to you, together with campaign materials for your solicitors.

I am looking forward very much to working with you and will be available to assist you in any way that I can.

With kindest regards,

Sincerely yours,

Name
Business Campaign Chairperson

Acknowledgment Postcard or Letter
(To be mailed to independent business workers as they are recruited.)

[NAME OF YOUR ORGANIZATION]
INDEPENDENT BUSINESS CAMPAIGN

We deeply appreciate your willingness to be a campaign
volunteer in our independent business campaign.

A campaign kit with complete instructions will be given
or mailed to you about [insert date] together with
subscription cards for the businesses for which
you have accepted responsibility. If you have any
questions, please call campaign headquarters at

_____

Your help is an important contribution to further our
work and we are grateful.

Your captain is: _____
(name)

_____
(address)

_____
(telephone number)

Instructions for Business Workers
Independent Business Campaign

As a business solicitor, you make an important contribution by giving your business and professional neighbors an opportunity to support the work of our vitally important program.

1. Please examine your worker's kit carefully. It should contain:
   - A complete list of your assigned prospects
   - A subscription card for each of your assigned prospects (notice the detachable receipts)
   - Subscription cards for new businesses at addresses assigned to you
   - Important educational literature for each of your prospects.
2. Try to cover all of your prospects on [insert date], which is the opening day of our campaign. You should make your own gift first, because this is something that your prospect often will ask about.
3. Give the owner or manager of each firm or office on your list their subscription card, and try to obtain the contribution on opening day. Give everyone an educational pamphlet whether or not he or she makes a contribution.
4. Later in the week, call back on the prospects who were unprepared to contribute during your first visit.
5. There are no specific amounts that you should ask for, other than a thoughtful, proportionate gift.
6. Please record your progress and other pertinent information on your assignment list and return this to your captain with your proceeds and subscription cards at the end of the drive.
7. Try to have your returns in the hands of your captain by [insert deadline].

Thank you again for your interest, cooperation, and support.

Campaign Headquarters:

[insert address]

CAMPAIGN CHAIRPERSON

Independent Business Campaign Organization Chart

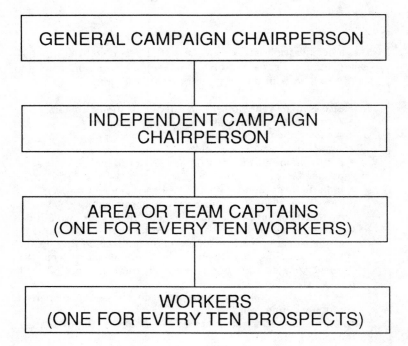

Contribution Card

All information except the worker's name should be filled in prior to solicitation. After the receipt is detached, the card should be returned to campaign headquarters.

The [name of organization] gratefully acknowledges receipt of your gift for the support of its program.

Date_____

Amount: $_____

Solicitor's
Signature: _____

INDEPENDENT BUSINESS CAMPAIGN

[Name of Organization]

Firm
Name: _____

Address: _____

Date: _____

Solicitor: _____

Gift: $_____

This card must be returned to Campaign Headquarters.

Fund-Raising Crusade Independent Business Report Form of the American Cancer Society, Inc.

Send this completed report to your Crusade Chairperson when your phase of the drive is concluded.

Number of independent business workers _____

Number of independent business blocks, arcades, and office buildings covered _____

Number and classification of gifts:

$500 and over _____ $5–24 _____

100–499 _____   1–4.99 _____

25–99 _____   Less than $1 _____

Total amount raised through independent business $_____

What was the independent business goal? $_____

Geographically, what percentage of the independent business area of the community was covered by this solicitation? _____

If all prospects were not solicited personally, was a supplementary direct mail solicitation made? If so, how many prospects were reached? _____

Please comment generally about the independent business acceptance, generosity, and reaction to the Cancer Crusade. Also tell of interesting experiences and things to repeat or guard against in future drives. _____

_____

_____

_____

MAIL SOLICITATION

*T*here is a reliable equation in any fund-raising program:

Personal solicitation = *more* dollars and *less* expense
Mail solicitation = *fewer* dollars and *more* expense

This is a negative way of getting into this topic, but there is so much competition for private sector contributions, and there has been such an enormous increase in mail solicitations, that most prospects are inundated and rarely read these appeals, let alone respond to them.

Now for the positive: For those prospects whom you are not able to solicit personally, obviously a letter campaign is better than no contact at all. Again, wherever possible, the signers should know the prospects, or should be known by them.

A great deal of marketing research has been done to learn some "do's" and "don'ts" of mail campaigns.

THE DO'S

- **Do** use a postage stamp where possible and hand-sign each letter.
- **Do** use your own stationery where possible.
- **Do** indicate in the opening paragraph why you are writing—your candor will be appreciated and will lend credibility to the appeal.
- **Do** enclose a piece of literature describing the goals, programs, needs, board members, financial statement, tax deductibility, etc.

- **Do** offer to provide any additional information that might assist the prospect in his or her deliberations.
- **Do** plan a follow-up, by telephone if possible, or write again asking if the prospect received your letter and if you can provide any further information that might expedite his or her consideration of your request.
- **Do** suggest a specific amount, proportionate to what you feel the prospect is capable of giving and proportionate to the project goal.
- **Do** indicate the various ways in which support can be given, such as cash, property, securities, or deferred gifts.

THE DON'TS

- **Don't** send a mimeographed letter.
- **Don't** use a signature stamp.
- **Don't** use an impersonal salutation such as "Dear Friend," "Dear Fellow Subscriber," or "Dear Fellow American."
- **Don't** use an envelope that does not show the identity of the sender. Some organizations believe that the recipient is less likely to open an envelope if it bears the name of a nonprofit organization. While a recipient may open such a letter out of curiosity, he or she may well resent the tactic.
- **Don't** enclose trinkets, mailing stickers, or other merchandise. (The recipient is under no obligation to return this, and the costs of these kinds of mailings are steep.)
- **Don't** be disappointed if the results of your mail campaign do not meet your expectations. (No one really knows what percentage of return is considered to be average or favorable.) Consider this as a cultivation step for future contact.

What You Can Do Tomorrow: Mail Solicitation

1. Ask your volunteers, including board members, if they would each identify ten prospects, from your lists or theirs, to whom they would write personal letters, on

their stationery, requesting thoughtful proportionate contributions. Then make follow-up telephone calls to those who have not replied within a reasonable time.
2. Clear all of the selections for possible duplications, so that a prospect does not receive more than one request.
3. Set up a timetable for follow-up reminders.

ALUMNI

*A*lumni play a unique and invaluable role in the development affairs of all educational institutions. At least, they have that potential. As quasi-official members of an institutional family, whose careers were enhanced by the education and training received at their alma maters, alumni are excellent prospects for support in any or all of the following areas:

- The annual fund
- The capital campaign
- The planned giving program.

In addition, they can be extremely effective as leaders and volunteers at all levels of the campaign organization. Many alumni turn in superb campaign performances, making major gifts of their own, and obtaining major support from fellow alumni, other individuals, corporations, and foundations.

In campaign settings, alumni work best within special divisions, functioning in uniformity with the other campaign divisions, following the same timetables, participating in all meetings, public relations programs, and special events, and operating under the direction of the general campaign chairperson.

Between campaigns, alumni associations traditionally conduct their own fund-raising programs within their own constituencies, on an annual or ongoing basis. Most of these programs follow similar organizational patterns, forming divisions based on graduating class, and designating alumni from each class as class agents, who also act as fund-raising coordinators.

Alumni associations also maintain organized chapters in geographic areas (region, state, city), where large numbers of alumni are located. This decentralization provides better settings for fund-raising, since prospective donors, both alumni and non-alumni, are more likely to respond to contacts made by local solicitors. Benefits and special events also are more likely to succeed when they are planned and presented by local alumni.

Alumni programs, however, are rarely successful when their only objective is to raise funds. In order for these programs to succeed, there needs to be an ongoing infusion of interest and involvement by the leadership of the organization. The following ten suggestions will help you to do this on an organized basis:

1. Make your board chairperson, president, or chief executive officer, deans, and certain faculty members available for speaking assignments at major alumni meetings.
2. Encourage the attendance of these individuals at alumni special events, such as seminars, lectures, exhibits, and benefits.
3. Place alumni on your mailing lists to receive annual reports, newsletters, and other organizational materials.
4. Invite alumni to all appropriate school events, such as commencement exercises, seminars, lectures, and open house tours.
5. Keep alumni informed of how the money they contributed was spent.
6. Invite alumni to visit their alma mater whenever they are in the vicinity and extend to them (and their families) every possible courtesy, consideration, and assistance with problems they may encounter in connection with lodging or travel.
7. Consider placing qualified alumni on appropriate official boards, committees, or advisory groups.
8. Encourage alumni sponsorship of special homecoming events.
9. Recognize, in an appropriate manner, alumni who have received special honors and awards in their respective fields.

10. Be alert to any other opportunity to make alumni know that their support is appreciated and important to your institution.

None of these suggestions will inspire very much enthusiasm, let alone support, from an alumnus who harbors negative memories of student years at an alma mater that did not seem to have any visible concern or interest in his or her personal well being. For this very good reason, the alumni program should begin on the first day of enrollment of the freshman class and continue through, and, of course, beyond, graduation.

One alumni program that serves as a good role model is currently in place at a midwestern university. Here are some of the highlights that make it unique and effective:

1. Alumni are woven into the fabric of the institution, serving on its board of trustees, administration, and faculty.
2. The board chairperson works closely with the president of the National Alumni Association Board and attends all of its meetings, as well as all major meetings and special events of alumni chapters throughout the United States.
3. The chairperson of the board personally hosts an annual homecoming weekend, and attends all of its scheduled events, together with solid representation from the board, administration, and senior faculty. These events include a reception, an educational seminar, a luncheon, tours of the school, a dinner dance honoring recipients of annual Distinguished Alumni Awards, and a farewell breakfast. At no time during this weekend is any reference made—directly or indirectly—to fund-raising or to institutional needs.
4. On the first day of enrollment of freshman students, a half day is devoted to an orientation program, where students are welcomed by the board chairperson, deans, and president of the National Alumni Association. At that time, a handsome clipboard is presented to each student as a gift from the alumni association.
5. Throughout the school, there is a significant display of alumni interest in student life, as evidenced by a splendid

exercise room and an attractive and comfortable student lounge equipped by the alumni association, and by alumni leaders' attendance at all major student events.

6. On the evening before graduation, the alumni association hosts a dinner dance for the graduating students and their families. At this time, the students are welcomed into the association by its president.

7. Within the alumni association, fund-raising is conducted quietly and effectively.

The sense of family and tradition, I'm sure, exists at many institutions. Ongoing interaction between school officials, students, faculty, and alumni can produce a kind of bonding that is manifested in the generous and ready response of alumni to the needs of their alma mater.

GOVERNMENT AGENCIES

A comprehensive development program would not be complete without an ongoing exploration of possible mutual interests with government agencies at all levels: federal, state, county, and municipal. This is a much-neglected but important source of funding for even the smallest organization whose programs fall within the sphere of government interests, which include virtually every area of philanthropy: health, education, welfare, civic, and cultural affairs.

Partnerships and working relationships between government and the private sector have existed for years, ranging from National Institute of Health grants for medical research to federal grants for numerous other kinds of programs. Many grants are made directly by federal, state, and local government, and the result is an enormously rich and productive relationship, which certainly warrants exploration by most nonprofit organizations and institutions.

In order to accomplish this, a government affairs chairperson should be appointed from within the board development committee to work with designated staff in achieving the following objectives:

- To identify from local directories all government agencies in particular program categories.
- To contact those agencies by telephone or letter to learn the names, addresses, and telephone numbers of the appropriate officials.
- To contact these officials and secure lists of those whose areas of interest seem to match those of the organization.

- To begin a dialogue with each of these individuals through any or all of the following ways:
  A. Visits to their offices
  B. Exchange of literature explaining one another's policies, guidelines, and programs
  C. Visits by them to the organization to tour the facilities and to see the programs in action.
- To inform staff and (faculty) of available grant opportunities and request that they prepare proposals within prescribed guidelines.
- To invite government officials to the organization's appropriate regular and special events.
- To keep appropriate government agencies regularly informed of the organization's progress and relevant happenings.
- To request officials to keep the organization closely informed of new regulations, guidelines, or opportunities for support and to be sure that all deadlines and other requirements are complied with.
- Finally, to be alert to all of the appropriate ways in which the organization can acknowledge, publicly and with appreciation, the support that it receives from government agencies.

Where possible, try to arrange to have government officials meet your recipients of grants, preferably in your program settings.

Remember that this type of public-private partnership is uniquely American and has a long history and tradition of working in the public interest.

ENDOWMENT FUNDING

*A*lthough many endowment grants are made through legacies and bequests, many other endowment grants to nonprofit organizations and institutions of every kind are made outright by individuals, foundations, corporations, and other organized groups.

In seeking and promoting endowment support, consider these sound guidelines:

1. Identify and document your endowment needs:
    A. *Unrestricted:* To strengthen your organization's financial base and to help ensure viability.
    B. *Restricted:* Faculty chairs, professorships, and fellowships; lectureships, seminars, and other academic or scientific events; library funds, loan funds, scholarships, concerts, publications, etc.
2. Indicate the amounts of grants necessary (with payment schedules) to establish named funds in each restricted endowment category.
3. Explain in detail the nature of endowment funding; the permanence of endowment funds, forms of recognition such as naming the funds in accordance with the donor's desire, placing appropriate names on buildings or units of buildings (libraries, dormitories, laboratories, classrooms, recreation areas, clinics, etc.), and in appropriate publications.
4. When you receive an endowment grant, acknowledge and recognize it publicly and privately in every appropriate manner:

A. Announcements to the news media
B. At special events (receptions, luncheons, etc.) organized expressly for announcement purposes, annual meetings, and written expressions of appreciation from a variety of high level officials of the organization.
C. Written expressions of thanks from those who will benefit from the endowment, including workers in endowed facilities, and scholarship and fellowship recipients. Where possible, arrange to have the donors meet the beneficiaries, preferably in their work settings or at a reception, luncheon, or other special event, hosted by the board chairperson or president of your organization.

5. Invite donors and their families to all special events such as lectures, concerts, seminars, workshops, exhibitions, etc., that are directly or indirectly supported by their endowed funds.

6. Make reports to donors on the earnings and regular expenditures of their funds.

7. Send donors copies of papers, articles, lectures, and books written by recipients of their support. Be sure that all of these publications include appropriate credit to the endowment fund.

8. Seize any other opportunities to remind donors of the importance of their support in terms of making possible significant contributions to the betterment of society in general and of human life in particular. Invite donors to your annual meetings, other organizational events that are not related to their endowment funds, and appropriate events held in the homes or clubs of board chairpersons or presidents specifically to honor and to give them special recognition.

MEMORIAL AND SPECIAL-OCCASION GIVING

Memorial gifts programs have been in effect for many years and are continuing to grow both in scope and in number. The American Cancer Society has been conducting such a program since 1947.

In recent years, many organizations who have achieved excellent results from their traditional memorial gifts programs have found it profitable also to include opportunities for special-occasion grants as a cofeature. The plans are simple and usually are conducted under the supervision of year-round volunteer chairpersons, with small committees to assist in the continual promotion of the project.

Because of the sensitive nature of memorial and special occasion giving, it is important that the highest standards of dignity, good taste, and restraint be observed as suggested in the following guidelines:

1. In all cases, the families of the deceased or honoree are notified of the contribution (and the contributor), without reference to the amount donated.
2. The donors receive receipts, which may be supplemented by letters of appreciation by appropriate officials of the organization.
3. In instances where a family has requested that memorial or special occasion contributions be sent to a particular organization, that organization may wish to express its appreciation in the form of a letter from an appropriate official.

There are a number of ways in which this program can be promoted, but the following standard procedure has proven to be effective for many organizations:

1. Provide a supply of appropriately worded coupon booklets to your volunteers for their personal use and to give to others.
2. Inform local clubs and organizations of your program and provide samples of your materials for their ordering and distribution.
3. Send annual mailings describing your program to these organizations, as well as to your contributors, local companies, churches, clergy, and other friends of your organization.
4. Set up special displays or exhibits in highly visible areas containing supplies of appropriate materials for interested individuals to take with them.
5. Send small supplies of booklets to past memorial and special-occasion donors for their convenience in making future gifts of this kind.
6. Include in your newsletters and other appropriate publications a special column describing your program and include a coupon that may be clipped for making a memorial or special-occasion gift.
7. Consider appropriate news releases describing your program.

There are many different kinds of forms that can be used for promoting, making, receipting, and acknowledging these gifts. The following set of forms may help you design forms that fit your situation.

Memorial Remittance Envelope

The envelope shown here can be used as a mailing or distribution piece to persons interested in making a memorial gift. The envelope is designed to be enclosed with the card of appreciation to the donor of the memorial gift for future contributions.

THE MEMORIAL GIFTS PROGRAM

A memorial gift to the American Cancer Society is a thoughtful gift—a living memorial. This tribute to someone loved means others are helped. Many individuals, organizations, firms, and other groups practice memorial giving regularly. These gifts support an increasingly large proportion of the American Cancer Society's program of Research, Education and Service.

Every gift provides material aid to the Cancer Research Program in laboratories and hospitals across the nation; helps educate the public to the importance of detecting cancer in time; and supports service programs for those stricken with the disease.

Every contribution is acknowledged with an official receipt to the donor and is tax deductible.

A memorial card is sent to the family of the deceased, with the name of the person honored, and the name or names of the donor. The amount of the gift is not indicated.

(Message may be printed on inside flap for promotional purposes.)

Suggested General Memorial Letter
(Clubs, Organizations and Industries)

Date _____

Dear _____:

Many recent requests for information about our memorial program prompted me to send you this letter.

When an employee (or a member of your club) dies of a particular disease, there is no better way to honor the departed one than to strike back at the disease which took this valued life. A memorial contribution will not only express the depth of your concern, but will also be used wisely through research, education, and service to put an end to the disease.

I am enclosing a leaflet which explains the simple procedures, and a self-addressed envelope. I think you will agree that "in memory" contributions are a fitting way to honor the memory of those we love.

Sincerely yours,

Enclosure

Suggested letter to be sent to the family of the deceased when they have requested that contributions be sent to the American Cancer Society

Date _____

Mrs. John L. Jones
Number and Street
City and State

Dear Mrs. Jones:

I wish to express to you the deep and grateful appreciation of the Society for suggesting that those who knew and loved your _____ make gifts in his memory to the never-ending work of the American Cancer Society.

It is only through such thoughtfulness that the vital efforts of the Society can go on, and I am sure that eventually, through research and intense effort, this menace to the health and well-being of so very many people will be met and conquered. You have helped to that end.

May I express our sympathy over your loss.

Sincerely yours,

(Signed by: Chapter Officer
or Memorial Chairperson)

Memorial Remittance Envelope

The envelope shown here can be used as a mailing or distribution piece to persons interested in giving a contribution to the memorial program. The envelope also is designed to be enclosed with the card of appreciation to the donor for future contributions.

THE MEMORIAL PROGRAM

A memorial gift to the American Cancer Society is a thoughtful gift—a living memorial. This tribute to someone loved means others are helped. Many individuals, organizations, firms and other groups practice memorial giving regularly. These gifts support an increasingly large proportion of the American Cancer Society's program of Research, Education and Service.

Every gift provides material aid to the Cancer Research Program in laboratories and hospitals across the nation; helps educate the public to the importance of detecting cancer in time; and supports service programs for those stricken with the disease.

Every contribution is acknowledged with an official receipt to the donor and is deductible for tax purposes.

A memorial card is sent to the family of the deceased, with the name of the person honored, and the name or names of the donor. The amount of the gift is not indicated.

Enclosed is a Memorial Gift in the amount of $_____

In Memory of _____
　　　　　　　　　Name

PLEASE SEND MEMORIAL CARD TO:

_____
Name

_____
Address

_____
City　　　　　　　　　　　　　　　Zone

FROM:　　　_____
　　　　　　Name

_____
Address

_____
City　　　　　　　　　　　　　　　Zone

Sample Memorial Gift Acknowledgment Forms

AMERICAN CANCER SOCIETY
Illinois Division, Inc.

𝔄 𝔆ontribution 𝔍n 𝔐emory of

𝔥as been receibed from

For Research • Education • Service

𝔄 gift on your behalf . . .

has been received by the American Cancer Society from

_____

_____

on the occasion of

_____

Sample Memorial Gift Contribution Forms

Name of Your Organization

I contribute the sum of

$ _____

in memory of
(in honor of)

_____

Please send an appropriate card to

_____
Name

_____
Address

From

_____
Donor's Name

_____
Address

Memorial Contributions are Tax Deductible.

COMMENT

You should be alert to the possibility of receiving large memorial contributions, which may require special handling and special acknowledgment. The donors of large contributions should be considered as prospects for expanded giving in other areas, and as sources of future volunteer leadership.

BENEFITS

*T*here are many kinds and variations of benefits, and every nonprofit organization should be aware of both the rewards and pitfalls of participating.

It is important, for example, that those who plan benefits, as well as those who support them, understand the federal income tax factors involved. Internal Revenue Service regulations stipulate that a charitable contribution cannot be fully deducted if any item or service was received in return for the contribution. This includes the kinds of perquisites available at any large fund-raiser—dinner, champagne, goody bags, a dance performance—and for many events the value of such perqs equals or exceeds the price of admission. The IRS allows deduction only of the amount not compensated for by goods or services and holds responsible not only the taxpayer, but also the nonprofit organization, which would have to calculate and reveal the fair market value of the goods or services.

All benefits fall within one of the following major categories, summarized below:

1. **Benefits conducted by volunteers and staff of the benefiting organization where all expenses are contributed or underwritten by individual or corporate "angels"** making it possible for 100 percent of the gross proceeds to go to the organization.

Comment. This type of benefit is highly desirable from every point of view. First, people are far more likely to purchase tickets to an event where they know that the full ticket price will go to the benefiting organization. Also, an organization's image and credibility are enhanced when it attracts sufficient support from one or two interested individuals (or corporations) to defray the cost of a benefit. Unless the benefactors request anonymity, it is extremely important—both to them and to the recipient organization—that their generous contributions be given maximum public acknowledgment.

2. **Benefits conducted by volunteers and staff of the benefiting organization with expenses paid from gross receipts.**

Comment. With this type of benefit, support may fall short of expectations, with the possible result that the proceeds may barely (or not even) cover expenses. Therefore, expenses must be reduced in every way possible. Many organizations solicit contributions of goods, services, facilities, food, entertainment, printing, promotion, public relations, cooking and service, and other items.

3. **Benefits conducted by one nonprofit organization on behalf of another,** such as church groups, service clubs, community organizations, or newspapers holding benefits with net profits (after expenses) going to another organization, described as a "passive recipient."

Comment. There are three positive factors about this type of arrangement:
  A. No commitment of funds or workers is required.
  B. Organizations who conduct such benefits usually have the experience and resources (including workers) to make them successful.
  C. Many people who would not normally contribute to your campaign would support a benefit held on behalf of your cause.

Because the name of your organization is used in the promotion of the benefit, you should request specific information describing the manner in which this benefit is to be organized and conducted, to ensure that it meets your standards of dignity.

4. **Benefits conducted on behalf of a nonprofit organization
   by a for-profit promoter or promotion firm** that normally
   works on a fee or commission basis. In these cases, the benefiting organization receives the net proceeds, after all expenses, fees, and/or commissions are paid.

Comment.   The net proceeds of a benefit event, mass mailing, collection, or other activity might be disappointingly small
because of the added expense of promotional fees or commissions, which, in some cases, can be outrageously high. An organization should exercise extreme caution before allowing its
name to be used as a beneficiary of a benefit over which it has
no control. Before entering into any commitment, the benefiting organization should have assurance that the promotion
of the event will be conducted in good taste and that the expenses will not be disproportionately high.

EVALUATION CRITERIA

The success of benefits should not be measured entirely by the
amount of money that they raise. Other criteria for evaluation
include the following:

1. Opportunities for dissemination of important information about your programs.
2. Amount of publicity generated.
3. Opportunities to interest new people in your organization, provided that the benefit atmosphere is warm and
   friendly, with a prevailing feeling of camaraderie.

Every organization must judge for itself the plusses and
minuses of each benefit that is being considered.
In a nutshell: If your contemplated benefit is not held too
close to the regular campaign period and is otherwise well
timed; if expenses can be held to a reasonable level; if the
nature of the event is within the boundaries of good taste; if it can
generate publicity; and if it can help to bring about greater public
awareness and understanding of your organization and its programs, then your benefit can be an extremely important supplement (but never a replacement) to the regular campaign effort.

GIFTS-IN-KIND

*T*he term "gifts-in-kind" is used to describe contributions of anything other than money or securities. These contributions generally can be divided into two categories:

1. **Donations made at the initiative of the contributor,** who later claims the allowable value of the gift as a deduction on a federal income tax return. Nonprofit organizations usually have policies regarding the acceptance or rejection of these donations. Considerations include the condition of the articles being offered, whether the organization has a need for them, whether they are easily marketable, and whether there are inappropriate restrictions that accompany certain contributions, such as property to be used for specific purposes.
2. **Donations of specific articles or services made in response to requests by nonprofit organizations.** Many corporations and independent businesses have proven to be excellent prospects for a wide variety of gifts-in-kind, including new and used furniture, office equipment, office fixtures, computers, motor vehicles, printing, and meeting places.

The response by the professional community likewise has been excellent, with free service provided frequently in a variety of fields, including law, accounting, advertising, public relations, investments, photography, design, and even medicine.

Many nonprofit organizations include in their board memberships representatives of certain professions and industries, to give them built-in expertise in necessary operational areas.

Before making costly purchases of furniture, furnishings, and equipment, and before retaining the expensive services of professionals, first explore the possibilities of securing these goods and services as gifts-in-kind.

SUPPLEMENTARY METHODS OF FUND-RAISING

Many organizations supplement their traditional campaign income by using a variety of other methods of fund-raising. Some of these methods can be highly productive, depending on the nature of the projects, their timing, and how they are promoted and managed. Even the best of these, however, should be regarded as *additions to* and not *substitutions for* proven, traditional fund-raising programs. The following supplementary methods are the most commonly employed.

"THONS"

Telethons, radio-thons, marathons (walk-a-thons), bike-a-thons, swim-a-thons, dance-a-thons, and others generally require a considerable amount of preparation, staffing, and promotion. In addition to the funds raised, this type of event has the potential to generate a great deal of publicity and public education. In the case of telethons, advance gifts usually are needed, and in this connection, good judgment should be used in deciding whether regular donors should be approached for pacesetting contributions to be announced on the air at the beginning or during strategic periods of the telethon. Corporate and business donors generally are aware of the advertising value of these public announcements of their support.

At the beginning of the project, everyone handling money should receive written instructions as to when, where, how, and to whom contributions should be submitted and reported. After the conclusion of the project, every participant, including the media, should be properly acknowledged and thanked, and every gift receipted and acknowledged.

MAILING UNORDERED MERCHANDISE

Mailing seals, and other merchandise, more often than not, is extremely costly, relatively unproductive, and seems to be meeting with growing resistance. Contributions guidance organizations correctly advise recipients of unordered merchandise that they are under no obligation to return such merchandise if they do not wish to contribute to the sender.

TAG DAYS

A tag day may be defined as a (designated) one-day-long collection of contributions by volunteer workers stationed in strategic locations where passersby place their gifts in coin canisters or in other appropriate receptacles, and receive a tag.

Permission to conduct tag days must be secured from local authorities. In many communities, the number of authorized tag days is limited. Tag days should be scheduled for the latter part of the campaign, when all of the regular solicitation has been completed.

Responsibility for the event should be assigned to a volunteer chairperson, appointed by the development committee of the board. The chairperson, in turn, should recruit a strong committee to assist, because tag days must be well staffed in order to cover all of the crowded centers in the community. The number of volunteers needed can be easily determined by the number of areas earmarked for coverage multiplied by the number of volunteers needed for each area, on the basis of each volunteer working a two- or three-hour shift.

The success of your tag day will depend greatly on publicity. You should request the help and support of media officials early, so that they have time to plan their announcement and coverage of the event. You should plan to order, well in advance of your tag day, all of the materials that you will need, such as coin canisters and identification badges for your workers, and tags and educational literature for contributors.

All coin canisters should be numbered and records kept of the volunteers to whom they are assigned. Be sure that every canister is accounted for and that the amounts collected are appropriately recorded. In certain crowded areas, a volunteer may fill his or her coin canister quickly. Have spotters, with extra empty cans, move from one area to another to replace materials, so as not to lose precious time and money.

Provide written instructions to everyone who is involved in handling money regarding the procedure for receipting any large gift that may be made, for reporting, and for submitting contributions.

Finally, make sure that appropriate letters of appreciation are sent to all of your volunteers, to the media, and to everyone else who provided assistance and support.

BOOTH CANVASS

In a booth canvass, contributions are collected during a specific period of time from passersby. Volunteers tend booths placed in strategic locations such as shopping arcades, malls, bus or train stations, and other public places, both indoors and out. Coin canisters or similar receptacles are used to collect contributions. The booth canvass can be another successful way to raise supplementary funds, with excellent additional benefits in the areas of publicity and public education. The following eight-point outline should help you plan, set up, and carry this project to a successful conclusion:

1. Begin with the appointment of a booth canvass committee chairperson by the development committee of the board.
2. The committee chairperson should divide the community into workable areas and recruit a booth chairperson for each area. The booth chairpersons, in turn, staff the area

with volunteers. Recommended sources of volunteers include regular volunteers of the organization and members of local clubs, organizations, and churches.

3. The booth chairperson should carefully determine the number of volunteers needed at each booth and the hours when they should be on duty. The average volunteer should be asked to work two- or three-hour shifts, during periods when traffic is heaviest.

4. Be sure that all booth canvass volunteers are thoroughly oriented and receive instructions in writing as to their specific duties, as well as information about the programs and needs of your organization.

5. Secure permission to place booths in the locations of your choice from the proper authorities: hotel lobbies, shopping centers, shopping malls, railroad stations, air terminals, department stores, banks, etc. Be prepared to provide the dates, the space, and the number of hours that each booth will be manned.

6. First determine carefully the type and quantity of materials you will need such as coin canisters, badges, and educational literature. Then place your order so that delivery can be made well in advance of the opening date of your booth canvass. All canisters should be numbered and records kept of the booths to which they are assigned, so that every canister can be accounted for. Keep careful records of the amounts collected.

7. Provide written instructions to all of the individuals manning the booths as to when, where, how, and to whom donations should be receipted, reported, and submitted.

8. Be sure that all volunteers, including donors of space, permissions, publicity, and other forms of support are appropriately thanked, and their assistance acknowledged. Finally, be sure that all of the booths and all of the materials stored therein are removed from the booth areas promptly and at the time and date agreed upon with the proprietors.

MEETINGS

*T*he nature and number of campaign meetings that are required will vary from one organization to another. However, every meeting should accomplish specific objectives, and every effort should be made to ensure maximum attendance, a comfortable setting, and an interesting, meaningful, and tight agenda.

Successful campaigns need good meetings to inspire, to inform, and to help sustain interest, visibility, and momentum. Meetings also provide deadlines for the completion of assignments.

TYPES OF MEETINGS

Meetings usually fall within two general categories: those that are held behind the scenes, and those that are public. Behind-the-scenes meetings to plan, organize, and deal with problems are especially important for campaign cabinets and other leadership combinations. They should be scheduled for times and intervals that are deemed appropriate by the general campaign chairperson and other key leaders. Equally important, traditional kickoff and report meetings are strongly recommended for every campaign.

The Kickoff Event

This event does not necessarily have to be a dinner or a luncheon—it should help to stimulate feelings of fellowship, pride in association, and obligation that inspires and motivates volunteers to tackle their assignments with vigor and enthusiasm. Kickoff events also generate publicity for the campaign.

The Report Meeting

Experience has proven beyond doubt that report meetings—spaced at intervals not too far apart—are essential for the three following reasons:

1. They provide deadlines for completion of assignments.
2. They help to evaluate progress.
3. They provide a setting for the identification of problems so that remedial action can be taken before these problems become compounded or insoluble.

FORMATS FOR MEETINGS

Many organizations begin their meetings with invocations and close them with benedictions, both given by members of the clergy, although, on occasion, laypersons also are called upon. For meetings that are attended by volunteers of different faiths, the following recommendations may help you avoid situations that some volunteers may consider to be offensive:

1. Divide the invocation and benediction duties among clergy from each of the major faiths, so that, during the course of the campaign, meetings are "balanced."
2. Indicate to your volunteers that this is the plan that will be followed.
3. Request all clergy delivering invocations and benedictions to make them ecumenical.

ELEVEN WAYS TO MAKE YOUR MEETINGS MORE SUCCESSFUL

1. Appoint a special events committee to take responsibility for the planning, organization, and implementation of all meetings and special events.

2. For smaller meetings, personalize each invitation. Salutations such as "Dear Committee Member" or "Dear Fellow Campaigner" do not encourage attendance. Signatures should be hand-signed. Many people will not read letters that bear signature facsimiles.
3. Include an RSVP card with every invitation so that you can be sure that everyone will be accommodated, and that you avoid waste of refreshments, space, and other overhead items.
4. Consider extending invitations to spouses or companions of invitees, especially for evening meetings. This is a good way to cultivate the interest of those who are close to the volunteer or to the prospect and who participate in decisions regarding volunteer service and contributions.
5. Arrange for follow-up telephone calls to all invitees who have not responded by a certain time.
6. Where appropriate, ask invitees who have indicated their inability to attend to send representatives in their places.
7. At the meeting, provide each attendee with a copy of the agenda and be sure that you follow that agenda.
8. In smaller meetings, introduce everyone in the room. In larger meetings, acknowledge those present, at least by campaign unit. Introduce major leaders and guests separately.
9. Provide maximum opportunities for as many people as possible to express themselves. Even the shyest individuals will respond to questions such as why they became interested, how they were recruited, and what meaningful experiences they have had as volunteers.
10. Indicate in the invitation when the meeting will begin and when it will end, and be sure that the schedule is observed. Luncheon meetings should be adjourned no later than 2 P.M., and dinner meetings on weeknights should be adjourned no later than 10 P.M. The image of your organization and future meeting attendance will be enhanced if you establish a tradition of beginning and ending your meetings at the times indicated. Early arrivals can be discouraged at best and demoralized at worst

when a meeting is delayed to await the arrival of latecomers. It is also inexcusable for meetings to extend far beyond their indicated adjournment times.
11. Prior to adjournment, observe the following priorities:
    A. Announce the time, date, and place of the next meeting.
    B. Ask those present if anyone has a final comment or question.
    C. Make appropriate acknowledgments of the fine work on the part of those who planned and arranged the meeting.
    D. Take the time to properly thank everyone for coming.

PROBLEM-SOLVING

The following formula may serve as a useful guide when you are planning a problem-solving meeting:

1. Identify the problem.
2. Gather data.
3. List possible solutions.
4. Test possible solutions.
5. Select the best solution.
6. Put the solution into action.

It has been said that you are halfway to a solution when you can write out a clear and accurate statement of the problem.

PUBLIC RELATIONS

*G*ood public relations involves the development and maintenance of good relations with whatever segment of the public you may wish to reach, including those in need of your services as well as those on whom you must depend for support. I do not believe there is any mystery in achieving effective public relations: It could well begin with a courteous and pleasant reception of a telephone call or in the cheerful and efficient rendering of a service, and certainly in the proper acknowledgment of contributions of time, money, or other gifts.

A good organization often is not given credit for what it does, simply because it has not effectively presented its program to the public. Likewise, poor communication is frequently the cause of problems that incorrectly are attributed to public apathy or to other unrelated causes.

IMAGE

"Image" is a word which one hears and reads about almost to a point of exhaustion, yet there is no other word which conveys quite the same meaning. Many organizations get into complex and expensive programs of image improvement. When these programs are unsuccessful, it is generally because the intelligence of the public is underrated and because images created by devices and gimmicks must be continually nourished by these contrivances. On the other hand, honestly appraising the reasons for a poor image is a great step forward in devising steps toward its correction.

There are only two reasons for an organization to have a poor image. One is the poor quality of its product; the other is a failure to effectively communicate information about the product. We are assuming, of course, an honest desire to correct existing imperfections in the "product" so that a good image then can be projected and communicated.

Some years ago, the author addressed a meeting of The Eye Bank Association of America, which, at that time, was experiencing a sharp decline in the number of corneas being donated for transplantation. A discussion with the late Leonard Heise, executive director of the affiliated Illinois Society for the Prevention of Blindness, revealed that many people believed it was sacrilegious to donate any part of their bodies.

In the ensuing discussion, the author recommended that the group consider asking clergy of the major faiths to confirm that the donation of corneas was not sacrilegious. He recommended further that the cooperation of the media be sought to help correct this image and to establish a new one constructed around the thoughtfulness and concern for others that characterized eye donors.

EXTERNAL PUBLIC RELATIONS

External public relations involves the competitive area of publicity and requires an understanding of the problems that the media face in trying to maintain a well-balanced public service program. It behooves every nonprofit organization to review its relationships with local communications executives to ensure that

1. they are aware of the existence of the organization, its programs, and its objectives;
2. the organization elicits the aid of local news editors and radio and TV station program managers in its planning;
3. the organization is aware of their needs. It is important, for example, to know about such things as press deadlines, what to include in news releases, the provisions of advance information to the media, and in properly calling attention to those activities which may invite feature coverage.

If you have further questions concerning publicity, why not ask the advice of those people who really know most about it? You will find that most local editors and TV and radio directors will cordially receive you and give you valuable guidance.

Are you keeping your accomplishments, activities, and needs before the public? Does the public know all of the ways in which they can help in your program? Do you hold regular informational meetings to which the public is invited? These questions may help you to gauge whether you are on a good wave length with your public.

SIX BASIC STEPS

Irving I. Rimer, public relations consultant and former vice president for public relations of the American Cancer Society, suggests these six basic steps to follow in establishing a sound public relations program.

1. *Research and analysis:* Using information from past surveys, formal or informal interviews with executive staff and board members, or discussions with members of the media and other community leaders, determine what is the public's image of the institution. What are the strengths and weaknesses in public attitudes? What kind of media support does the organization enjoy? Where are the pockets of resistance to the organization? What do the volunteers know about the organization's achievements, current programs, and plans for the future? What are the elements of the program or services which lend themselves best to campaign promotions? Answers to these questions provide the public relations component with guidelines to formulating a basic program for the appeal.
2. *Planning public relations strategy:* Decide the tone and tenor of the communications. Where will the human interest and emotional content be focused? What will be the theme or slogan to dramatize the overall appeal in all messages? The slogan of the National Negro College Fund, "A Mind Is a Terrible Thing to Waste," is used year after year because it

sets the purpose of the basic campaign. Decide if your campaign should rely heavily on mass media or if you need to use more specialized channels to reach prospects and key publics. What should be the nature of advertising? Should this be public service or paid? What materials will be needed? What will be needed to offset competition from similar organizations? Answers to these questions will provide direction and quality to the strategy employed.

3. *Proper organization of the public relations program:* Because no public relations program can succeed without proper organization, determine who should direct the effort. Will additional staff be necessary? Should a public relations committee of experts in communication and advertising help advise on the campaign or even enter into operations? How should news be covered within the institution to feed the publicity? What kind of budget will be necessary to sustain the operation?

4. *Time schedule:* Chronologically map the development of all publicity materials, events, releases, week by week and month by month. Definite periods should be fixed for such things as internal communications with key constituents, preparation of campaign brochures and backgrounders, and creation of spots. This eliminates surprises and keeps the total campaign organization alerted to all public relations developments.

5. *Operations:* Now that the strategy has been deployed, an organization established, and a time table set, the public relations program moves into operation. Crises may occur, complaints and criticism from prospects and others may arise, or a need for new approaches may come up. In order to be prepared for any of these situations you must sustain a close working relationship between the public relations component and others in the fund-raising organization. Equally important, the public relations staff must have direct access to top management on a day-to-day basis. Public relations staff need to be up front with others and clear their concepts, designs, and materials with others. Harmony is essential.

6. *Evaluation:* Following the campaign, evaluate the key elements of the public relations program. Did the theme work?

Was the advertising effective? Was the media coverage adequate? Was the time schedule followed? What worked? What didn't? What should be done next year to improve on the campaign? Many other questions follow in the course of this process.

IMPLEMENTING THE PROGRAM

Once your public relations program has been established and all of its basic issues resolved, use the following plan for implementing your program.

I. **Permanent (Long-range) Objectives**

A. Establish and maintain an institutional image of excellence and promise that properly reflects the quality of your organization.

B. Effectively communicate, to all of your constituencies and publics, the objectives, programs, and achievements of your organization.

C. Maintain a public awareness of how your programs directly affect the health and well-being of society.

D. Maintain an identity as an organization that richly merits support from both the private and public sectors.

E. Keep the organizational family fully informed on all aspects of the growth and development of your organization.

II. **Immediate Objectives**

A. Establish and maintain a system of regular communication to all of your constituencies and your publics of the leadership that the organization and members of its official family have provided and are providing in your particular program areas. Such a system should be designed to keep your organization's goals and priorities in the public view. This communication can be achieved only by ensuring that a steady flow of information involving the entire organization is regularly assembled, evaluated, and reported through proper channels to your public relations department, which, in turn, should be responsible for the communication of this information to all of the appropriate media.

B. Prepare these materials for the fund-raising campaign:

1. Case statement

2. Basic campaign brochure

3. Other material as deemed necessary

C. Generate and maintain high visibility for the campaign.

III. Procedure

A. Establish an ongoing system of procurement, assembly, and evaluation of information from the institutional family.

1. Provide forms through channels for selected members of the board of trustees, program executives, faculty, woman's board, alumni, and any other official body that accommodates the reporting of potential news items, including new objectives, new programs, special events, honors, awards, publications, grants, scientific or academic achievements, lectures, new appointments, promotions, and other activities of interest.

2. Distribute and return these forms through channels so that appropriate organization officials have an opportunity to review and evaluate the information submitted. Accordingly, they can screen out any items they consider inappropriate and forward the approved material to the public relations department. Individuals submitting inappropriate material should be informed of the reasons why subject material was edited. A sample news reporting form and a flow chart illustrating how news items are processed follow.

Sample News Item Reporting Form

Date _____

Name _____

Department and Position _____

Home Address (for local papers) _____

New Position or Promotion _____

New Publication _____

New Professional or Civic Honor or Award _____

_____

Other Activity or Special Event (Open House, Invitation to Lecture, New Program, Research Grant, Research Achievement, etc.)

_____

_____

_____

Community, Home Town, or Professional Publications to which you would like releases sent

_____

_____

_____
Signature
(Individual Submitting the Report)

_____
Signature
(Appropriate Designated Official)

Processing of News Items Submitted for Release to Media

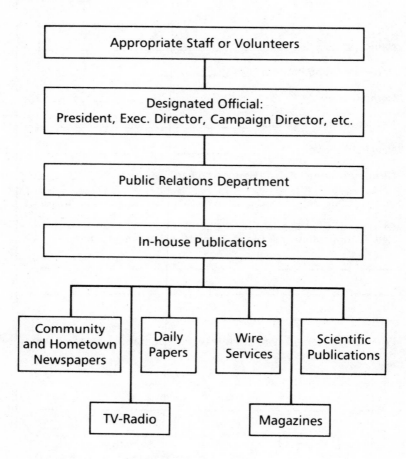

B. Establish methods of communication

1. Regular news releases

2. Development and placement of feature stories in newspapers, magazines, radio, and television

3. Television and radio appearances by organization and campaign leaders

4. Special events, including news conferences

5. Regular and special organization publications

6. Professional publications

C. The text of every news release about a particular individual prepared by your public relations department should be cleared, whenever possible, with the individual or individuals concerned.

D. Copies of all news releases should be sent back through channels for the information of those concerned.

IV. Contacts with the News Media

A. Contacts with the media should be initiated and maintained only by your public relations department.

B. Members of your organization who are approached by representatives of the news media should clear such requests through channels prior to giving interviews or making appearances on radio or television programs. Wherever possible, volunteers should be featured, and staff remain in the background. The one exception to this rule is the chief executive officer, who should be given appropriate publicity whenever possible.

V. Schedule for Reporting

A. News item reports should be submitted as soon as the event, activity, honor, or discovery is known. This helps your public relations department meet deadlines, maintain a steady flow of fresh information to all of your "markets," and have ready a rich reservoir of significant material for your own publications.

B. Have the public relations department give special treatment to those items that are judged to be of unusual interest or importance.

C. Maintain a steady flow of information to the news media, including releases that may not be published. This helps to identify and establish your organization as an important resource for future articles, features, and documentaries.

This chapter presents the subject of public relations from a general perspective and will not apply to every organization. I hope, however, it will serve as a useful resource to assist you in tailor-making the kind of specific public relations program that will best fit the needs of your organization.

ROLE OF GOVERNING BOARD MEMBERS IN FUND-RAISING

*T*he basic responsibility for fund-raising rests with the board, as does the responsibility for every other program or activity of the nonprofit organization. Accordingly, board members formulate the fund-raising policies and plans of the organization, and, through its committee or council on development, oversee the implementation of those policies and plans. However, the extent to which board members become involved in actual fund-raising varies with each individual. Some will contribute more than others. Some will participate actively in fund-raising. Some will not. It must be remembered that the *principal* role of a board member is not to raise funds.

Board members may choose to become involved in the fund-raising programs of their institutions in a number of ways:

- By making contributions commensurate with their abilities.
- By taking active leadership roles on the fund-raising team.
- By assisting in the recruitment of volunteers at various levels, ranging from chairpersons of campaign units to workers (solicitors).
- By identifying major gifts prospects.
- By bringing these prospects to organizational headquarters, campuses, and other program sites to view the settings, meet key people, and see the organization in action.
- By contributing through wills, bequests, and other forms of planned giving, and encouraging others to do the same.

- By being alert to ways in which they can express appreciation to volunteers and donors.
- By helping the development program to secure the understanding and support of the power circles in each of the publics from which support is necessary.
- By projecting the image of the organization through the interpretation of its structure, programs, goals, and achievements.

ROLE OF PARENTS IN FUND-RAISING

*T*he involvement of parents of current and former students generally should be planned and coordinated by a parents' association that should be represented on the school development council.

While the nature and extent of individual parent participation will vary, every parent can play an important role in a school's development program in one or more of the following ways:

- By providing direct financial support.
- By contacting other parents and/or friends for contributions.
- By helping to identify and develop sources of special support in the areas of legacies, bequests, and other forms of planned giving.
- By projecting the image of the school through the interpretation of its structure, programs, goals, and achievements.

Meaningful assistance from this potentially rich source of support depends on continued cultivation, effective communication, and good leadership by the parents' association.

Every parent is entitled to, and should receive the following:

1. Invitations to appropriate meetings and special events of alumni and other groups of the institution when held in areas near the parents' hometowns
2. Frequent, straightforward information about the institution, its progress, and its plans
3. Information about fee payments and tuition deadlines

a month in advance so that they can make necessary plans and provisions for payment
4. Advance information about orientation, parents' weekends, vacation periods, and campus events of interest so that they can plan to participate

Parents' associations can be extremely effective in channeling the talents, interests, and resources of parents into an effective, continuing force for the advancement of the institution. Like alumni associations, however, they will fail if their only purpose is to raise money. Many parents' associations have working committees on parent-college communications, student recruitment, public relations, orientation and student affairs, as well as the parent fund.

Development officers, deans, and other institutional officials should be actively involved in assisting and interacting with officers and boards of parents' associations.

COMMENT

The interests and objectives of different associations vary. Some select certain projects for support, such as faculty salaries, financial aid for students, and expansion or construction of capital resources, while others prefer unrestricted contributions that help underwrite operating costs. Expressions of appreciation to parent contributors and to parent associations should be commensurate with the level of support provided.

The interests of parents do not necessarily stop with the graduation of their children, especially those who have been contributors. They should be regarded and treated like all other past donors, with continued efforts made to obtain their continued, and in some instances expanded, support.

ROLE OF FACULTY IN FUND-RAISING

*T*he understanding and enthusiastic support of the faculty is crucial and should be planned and coordinated by a special faculty committee, which in turn should be represented on the school development council.

While the nature and extent of individual faculty participation will vary, every faculty member can assist in one or more of the following ways:

- By providing direct financial support
- By helping to identify and/or develop sources of regular or special support
- By interpreting the school's structure, programs, and objectives to students, to the local community, and to the community at large
- By serving as informational resources when called upon, particularly in cases of tours, special visits to the school by major prospects, and discussions concerning grants for the academic programs.

ROLE OF THE PRESIDENT OR CHIEF EXECUTIVE OFFICER IN FUND-RAISING

*T*he president or chief executive officer is the key player in the development program of any organization. He or she is the chief image-maker and fund-raiser, sometimes accompanying board members on major gifts missions or making the calls alone.

The president plays a predominant role in keeping the fund-raising operation alive, through ongoing communication with board members, other volunteers, alumni, faculty, prospective donors, and students. The president or CEO should be a familiar face on the television screen, in newspapers, and in campaign literature.

The president or CEO is responsible for the setting of goals and priorities. He or she also manages the budget, selects competent staff for the development department, and oversees all of the administrative elements of the fund-raising support system. He or she interacts with campaign leadership, board members, and alumni, providing inspiration and assistance whenever and wherever possible.

Also where possible, he or she brings major gift prospects into the institution through appointments to the governing board and advisory committees. The president or CEO should be alert to opportunities for cultivation of prospective major donors by inviting them to appropriate social events. He or she is involved in the design of major proposals which match the known interests of major donors.

The relationship between the president and the governing board has been compared to a good pair of scissors that needs two blades, working together and keeping each other sharp.

ROLE OF ALUMNI IN FUND-RAISING

*T*he leadership and support of the alumni is crucial to educational fund-raising. Formal involvement of alumni should be planned and coordinated by an official committee, which in turn should be represented on the school's development council, campaign cabinet, and any other major campaign body.

While the nature and extent of individual alumni participation will vary, each can assist in one or more of the following ways:

- By providing direct financial support (through the alumni campaign committee)
- By making planned (deferred) gifts to the school
- By helping to identify and/or develop sources of regular or special support within the alumni association or in the community at large
- By agreeing to contact some of these prospects personally
- By interpreting the school's structure, programs, and objectives
- By serving as informational resources when called upon.

SECTION IV

Post-Campaign

CLEANUP

*A*t the conclusion of virtually every campaign, after the final report meeting and whether or not the goal was reached, there are inevitably a number of prospects who have not yet responded to proposals or who were not called upon during the campaign.

Too often, the general cleanup practice is to send letters to all of these outstanding prospects announcing that the campaign is coming to an end, and urgently requesting their contributions. Some of these letters refer to emergent needs and the danger of reducing or eliminating certain programs and services if those needs are not met. The response to this type of mass mailing generally is poor.

Most organizations have found it profitable to formally extend their campaigns for short periods of time—usually between two and four weeks. This provides time to quickly regroup those volunteers who express a willingness to make follow-up calls on their outstanding prospects, or on other prospects. This also allows time for the formation of a plan of action by campaign leaders that includes the following elements:

1. A regrouping of those volunteers who have prospects still outstanding, requesting that they complete their assignments before the new deadline date.
2. Requesting volunteers who have already completed their own assignments to solicit a number of additional prospects, of their own choosing, who were not contacted by anyone. Contribution cards, bearing the names of these prospects, should be sent to the workers, together with adequate supplies of campaign literature and warm letters of appreciation from chairpersons.

3. Personal letters can be sent from the chairperson to prospects who are still unassigned, announcing the extension, the amount raised to date, the amount still needed to reach the goal, the reasons why it is important that the goal be reached (to continue or expand programs and services), and appealing for their support. The letters should include an invitation to visit the organization or to meet with the writer in another setting to discuss the campaign or the programs in more detail.
4. Where possible, a telephone follow-up can be made to prospects who have not replied to the appeal letter.

At this point the leadership should seek the cooperation of the media to publicize the extension of the campaign and to carry stories describing the importance of the organization's programs and services.

During the cleanup period, special attention should be given to former donors who are still outstanding. Contacts to these individuals should be made by appropriate unit chairmen.

Some organizations have found it effective to recruit new volunteers both from within and outside the organizations to conduct necessary cleanup activities, operating on the premise that a fresh infusion of interest and enthusiasm is needed. It is strongly recommended that campaign rallies be held prior to any cleanup solicitations, so that new volunteer forces can receive final instructions, appropriate additional supplies of campaign materials, and all of the inspiration and motivation that the organization's leaders can provide.

After all of your cleanup activities have been completed, be sure that all of your leaders and workers are adequately thanked and that final campaign totals are reported, internally and publicly through news releases. Whether the extended campaign has been successful or not, a special luncheon hosted by the chairperson of your board for key volunteers who performed above and beyond the call of duty can give your organization an additional opportunity to express appreciation to these key individuals.

REWARDS AND RECOGNITION

*T*he first step in preparing for your next campaign is to acknowledge, in a meaningful way, all contributions of money and volunteer services that were made in the current drive. Be sure to include everyone who has helped in any way: media officials, public officials who have issued proclamations or other forms of endorsement, clerical workers, etc.

All contributions should be acknowledged routinely by printed confirmations of receipt, containing an expression of thanks and bearing a signature facsimile of the general campaign chairperson. Major contributions and all volunteer services should be acknowledged by warm, personal, hand-signed letters from the general chairperson. Optional, but highly recommended, are additional letters, also personalized, from other officials of your organization, such as committee, division, or unit chairpersons, the board chairperson, or the chief executive officer. In cases of major contributions to a college or university, and especially in cases of endowment funding, appropriate faculty members or even students who receive assistance from a particular endowment fund could send letters of thanks to the donor.

In addition to the basics, here are ten forms of acknowledgment that have proven to be helpful in cultivating continued support from major donors and volunteers:

1. Telephone calls from appropriate chairmen.
2. Invitations to special events where awards and other appropriate expressions of appreciation are made.

3. Invitations to be special guests at other interesting events, such as open houses, graduation ceremonies, lectures, and program presentations.
4. Placing all donors and volunteers on your mailing list for newsletters, annual reports, and other appropriate publications.
5. Inviting certain major donors to become involved in your organization as leaders in fund-raising or other program areas.
6. Promoting outstanding volunteers to leadership assignments, not only in fund-raising, but also as members of governing or advisory boards, special committees, etc.
7. Listing contributors (not the amount of the gifts) and volunteers in your annual report and/or in other publications (after securing their permission to do so).
8. Inscribing the names of major donors and volunteer leaders on plaques prominently displayed on walls of appropriate buildings, laboratories, libraries, lounges, classrooms, and other facilities.
9. Awarding appropriate mementos ranging from lapel badges, pins, and other insignia-bearing paraphernalia. More expensive items, such as paper weights, cuff links, and neckties sometimes are given by the campaign chairperson as personal expressions of appreciation to key volunteers and major donors. Chairpersons also often host thank-you luncheons or dinners for key volunteers at their homes, hotels, clubs, or restaurants.
10. Inviting major donors and volunteers to appropriate groundbreaking and dedication ceremonies of facilities that were made possible by their contributions.

COMMENT

There may be still other forms of acknowledgment that you may select in constructing the type of thank-you program that best fits the needs of your organization. The nature and extent of each acknowledgment should match the size of the contribution or the magnitude of the volunteer's participation.

EVALUATION

*T*he critical importance of evaluating your fund-raising efforts cannot be emphasized too strongly. A diligent and thorough job of identifying the things that worked and the things that didn't will be invaluable in enabling you to refine, amend, or reconstruct your development program in your planning for the coming year.

Actually, evaluation is conducted in two stages. The first consists of an ongoing process that is in effect throughout the course of any fund-raising activity. Efficiently managed campaigns are continually evaluated while in progress to determine weaknesses that can be corrected before they become compounded and cause severe breakdowns in the entire operation. In addition to taking swift remedial action, the staff campaign director should carefully record these weaknesses so that preventive measures can be incorporated into plans for subsequent campaigns.

The staff campaign director should also bring problems to the attention of appropriate volunteer leaders for analysis and joint, swift remedial action. Regular report meetings enable campaign leaders to quickly identify and evaluate progress and problems on a periodic basis with relatively short intervals in between.

The second stage of the evaluation process traditionally takes place—or should take place—immediately after the campaign (or the fiscal year) is over. It is important to begin the process immediately, while the relevant information, perceptions, and insights are fresh in the minds of key volunteers and staff.

A well-planned evaluation process, in addition to providing a strong foundation for future planning, gives the volunteer force an opportunity to express their views and opinions regarding the recently completed campaign, and to share their recommendations with the organization's board and staff. Even if certain volunteers choose not to express their feelings, they still appreciate the fact that they are being recognized and their opinions valued.

There are two elements in the process of gathering the kind of comprehensive and reliable information upon which a dependable evaluation can be based. They are both important, but they must be accomplished in sequence: the evaluation form and the evaluation meeting.

PART I: THE EVALUATION FORM

The first step is to obtain the feedback and input of the entire volunteer force through the distribution and collection of evaluation form questionnaires. The questions on this form should be carefully thought out, limited to the items that are relevant, and clearly constructed so that they can be easily answered. They should also be set up so that the responses can be easily documented.

The questions on evaluation forms will necessarily vary from one campaign to another. However, some basic questions should be considered for inclusion on every form, and the form itself should be accompanied by a warm letter from the campaign chairperson, as illustrated in the sample.

PART II: THE GENERAL CAMPAIGN EVALUATION MEETING

The evaluation meeting should be held after the evaluation forms have been tabulated, reviewed, and summarized for presentation by the general campaign chairperson and the staff campaign director. This meeting should be called and chaired by the campaign chairperson or the chairperson of the board's development committee.

Sample Evaluation Questionnaire

TO: All volunteers in the 19-- _____ campaign

FROM: [Name]
         General Campaign Chairman

I want to thank you again for your interest, cooperation, and your fine performance in our campaign.

We are now in the process of putting together an official evaluation of the campaign, which will be based largely on the experiences, opinions, and recommendations of our splendid volunteer force, of which you are an important member.

The enclosed Evaluation Form is intended for your convenience in providing us with a summary of your views and suggestions regarding any and every part of our campaign operation. It is very important that you return this form in the self-addressed stamped envelope before [date]. [The date should allow the recipient at least three weeks to complete the questionnaire.]

Your views will be incorporated with those of our fellow volunteers and will be of great help in our planning for next year.

With kindest regards,

_____
[personal signature of general chairperson]

NOTE: Completion of this form is optional. If you choose not to fill it out, please return the blank form in the envelope provided.

Invitation List

The invitation list should include the following:

1. Chairperson of the governing board
2. Members of the board's development committee
3. All members of the campaign chairperson's cabinet (chairperson of the major campaign units)
4. Other key volunteer leaders selected by the chairperson and the staff campaign director
5. Chief executive officer
6. All members of the campaign staff

Evaluation Form

1. What was your specific campaign assignment (how many prospects), and how many dollars were you able to raise?
2. How were you enrolled? By whom?
3. Did you receive a written description of your responsibilities?
4. How were you oriented?
5. What campaign meetings did you attend?
6. Do you have any comments about these meetings?
   Did they help you?
   How could they have been improved?
   Were you introduced, either individually or together with your campaign unit?
7. How would you evaluate the campaign materials that were provided?
   The brochure?
   Program information?
   Campaign Instructions?
   Other?
8. Did you have enough material?
   _____ yes
   _____ too much
   _____ not enough
9. What recommendations do you have for the improvement of our campaign materials?
10. Was your immediate chairperson helpful to you?
    Did he or she ever contact you personally during the campaign to see how you were doing?
11. Was the campaign staff helpful to you?
12. Was someone at campaign headquarters always available when you called?
13. Did you feel that the campaign received good publicity support?
    Comments
14. Did you find that your prospects seemed to have a good image of our organization—including those who did not contribute?
15. Did your prospects ask you any questions that you were unable to answer?
16. Did you feel that you were adequately thanked for your efforts? Did you feel that your work was really appreciated?
17. Would you please comment on any other aspect of the campaign that either impressed you or disappointed you?
18. Based on your experiences, would you volunteer again for a future campaign if asked?

_____
Signature of Volunteer
(with campaign assignment)

Agenda

There are a number of different ways in which this meeting can be conducted so that everyone's input can be obtained, shared with one another, and summarized for later incorporation into a set of recommendations to be considered in the planning of next year's campaign.

In planning an agenda that will best fit your situation, consider the following items in the sequence suggested:

1. Introduce everyone present, identifying both their campaign and business titles and affiliations.
2. Thank everyone again for their dedicated efforts in the campaign and for their willingness to participate in this important evaluation process.
3. Explain the objectives of this meeting: to evaluate the past campaign and to make recommendations for future planning.
4. Distribute copies of the tabulations of the evaluation forms, and ask the campaign chairperson or the staff campaign director to present any pertinent observations and summaries that appear relevant, prior to discussion of the tabulations by the group.
5. Review all of the statistics and written comments, as summarized, and allow ample time for discussion and recommendations. Be sure that all of the pertinent comments and recommendations are documented for later review and consideration by the board's development committee and campaign staff.

Conflicting Views

If there are conflicting views regarding any part of the general discussion, the chairperson should remind the parties involved that each of his or her opinions will be recorded for later consideration. It should be clearly understood that the purpose of this meeting is to identify issues and make recommendations, not to make decisions or reach a consensus on any of these issues.

After the Meeting

Immediately following the evaluation meeting, the staff campaign director should begin to identify potential key leaders, beginning with the general campaign chairperson, for presentation to the board's development committee. Volunteer leaders who performed well in the past campaign should be considered for reappointment by chairpersons of the appropriate campaign units.

This process cannot begin until the general campaign chairperson (of the next year's campaign) has been recruited. Accordingly, the campaign director, the board chairperson, and the board's development committee chairperson should meet to identify and to recruit this important individual.

Future Planning

As soon as the general chairperson has been recruited and oriented, the leaders, as a group, should assemble to begin making general plans for next year's campaign, incorporating, selectively, the recommendations made at the evaluation meeting while they are still fresh in everyone's thoughts.

Additional information that this key committee may wish to consider includes the following:

1. Extent of board involvement in the past campaign. What percentage served as volunteers? What was the average contribution from board members? What was the total amount raised by board members, including their own gifts and gifts obtained from others?
2. Average contribution from the individual major gifts unit, corporations, foundations, and other campaign units.
3. The percentage of contributions that were made by past donors.
4. The percentage of contributions received, compared to turndowns.

These planning meetings should continue until the general campaign plan has been formed and approved by the governing board.

Cabinet Meeting

When the general campaign chairperson has completed the recruitment of chairpersons for each of the major campaign units, a meeting of this cabinet and the staff campaign director should be held to set up an ongoing evaluation process for the coming campaign, including evaluations of every campaign meeting; of the campaign literature, both when the volunteers receive the material and later when they can assess its value; the quality of the publicity as a cultivating and supporting service; the help that volunteers are getting, or not getting, from appropriate volunteer and staff leaders; and any other element or issue of the campaign. A supply of suitable forms (with stamped return envelopes) should be provided to every worker as part of the campaign kit.

PART III: THE CAPITAL CAMPAIGN EVALUATION MEETING

When a capital campaign has been concluded, a special evaluation meeting should be called by the chairperson of the board's development committee to consider ways in which the organization can capitalize on the good things that have resulted from the campaign. This meeting should include the general campaign chairperson, the chairperson of the planned giving division, the chairperson of the public relations committee, and the campaign staff.

Among the items that should be considered at this meeting are the following:

1. Reevaluation of any capital goals that have not been met, with a view toward including them in a long-range development program, together with operating and endowment needs.
2. Identification of volunteers who worked in the capital campaign, and who might be interested in continuing their service in the long-range development program.
3. Reactivation of an effective planned gifts program.

4. Continuation of a comprehensive public relations program to keep the public (external and internal) informed of progress, new objectives, and relevant events.
5. Organization of a special giving club, commonly known as associates, if one does not already exist. Membership in this group usually is limited to individuals who make annual contributions of whatever minimum is felt to be appropriate, such as $5,000, $1,000 or $500.
6. Reactivation of any element of a long-range development program that may have slowed down or stopped during the capital campaign, such as alumni, parents of students, parents of alumni, trust officers of banks, lawyers, accountants, or insurance executives.

SECTION V

Conclusion

CONCLUSION

*I*n writing this book, my principal objective was to compile all of the many elements of fund-raising, describe them in detail, and explain their relationships to one another. This book is intended to serve as a handbook and a guide for both campaign veterans and newcomers. Because of this, the contents of the book are limited to those policies, techniques, principles, methods, and procedures that may guide in the planning, preparation, and implementation of your fund-raising operation.

REASONS WHY SOME CAMPAIGNS FAIL

Even one negative element can play an important role in causing the failure or breakdown of an entire campaign. But most negative elements can be discovered easily, in the early stages of the campaign, while they are still correctable or remedial.

Summarizing below are twelve major reasons why some campaigns fail.

1. A poorly designed, poorly documented case for support.
2. Ineffective leadership, whose commitment at the time of recruitment did not include the traditional responsibilities of campaign chairpersons. In most of these instances, the major method of solicitation is by letter.
3. A poorly constructed and poorly designed campaign plan, which excludes the necessary elements of volunteer recruitment, orientation, and personal solicitation. In these instances, fund-raising is sporadic and may depend

on such methods as benefits, coin cans, and an assortment of events without specific goals and comprising collections rather than traditional campaign operations.

4. Lack of an operational timetable or failure to adhere to one.

5. Inadequate prospect identification and research, often resulting in an insufficient number of prospects, many of whom have no interest in supporting the campaign. This can be very discouraging to volunteers who experience a stream of rejections and begin to doubt the organization's public acceptance. Foundation directories, corporate directories, chambers of commerce membership rosters, and club membership lists used indiscriminately as sources for prospect lists often result in expensive and generally unproductive mailings. The principal cause of this problem lies in the failure to identify the organization's logical markets, and to develop lists of prospects within those markets.

6. Lack of public interest resulting from a failure to generate a vigorous external and internal publicity program that calls attention to the importance of the organization's programs.

7. Arbitrary assignment of prospects, resulting in mismatches between volunteers and prospects. In these instances, a simple rearrangement of assignments, allowing volunteers to select prospects when possible and permitting volunteer input into mandatory assignments, can make the difference between success or failure.

8. Poor or inadequate campaign materials that emphasize the price tag and not the product. This, together with inadequate or no orientation renders the volunteer incapable of making a compelling approach to a prospect, or answering questions regarding the organization's missions.

9. Lack of thoughtful and proportionate giving.

10. Mathematical fund-raising: Planning on reaching a goal by securing average amounts from each prospect, for example, if the goal is $200,000 and the prospect list numbers 4,000, saying "all we need is $50.00 from each prospect." The obvious fallacy is that people do not, cannot, and will not all give the same amount.

11. Unrealistic reliance on publicity alone to raise money.

Publicity is valuable in cultivating interest, helping to secure recognition, and attracting a few contributions. However, irrespective of how much publicity your campaign receives, it cannot take the place of the traditional fund-raising operation. People who give money generally do so only when they are asked.

12. General apathy or lack of enthusiasm on the part of the organization's top leadership probably is the most important reason why campaigns fail. This includes lack of urgency, lack of excitement, lack of anything that would inspire anyone to respond to a call for volunteers or that would motivate a volunteer to do his or her best work and make a thoughtful contribution.

WHY SOME CAMPAIGNS SUCCEED

Following are eleven very important elements in a successful campaign. While some are considered to be more important than others, in fact, like the links in a chain, they are of equal importance.

1. A sound case, well documented, that has public acceptance.
2. A well-constructed and well-conceived campaign plan.
3. Top leadership of quality and dedication, who, in turn, have recruited and oriented sufficient numbers of highly motivated volunteers to personally contact all of the prospects necessary.
4. A well-researched and rated list of prospects, selected by, or assigned to, volunteers of equal stature.
5. A carefully followed timetable.
6. An efficient system for record keeping and reporting.
7. A vigorous and ongoing support program of publicity and special events.
8. Staunch support from the governing board.
9. Interesting, inspirational, and informational meetings for purposes of kickoffs, reports, orientation, and special events.
10. Sound management of the entire campaign operation by the general chairperson and the staff campaign director,

and ready support and assistance whenever and wherever it was needed.

11. An atmosphere of excitement, urgency, enthusiasm, and universality. Requests for support must be made proudly and boldly. Prospects must be asked to join the volunteers in helping to do something meaningful about those problems, situations, or issues that require their investment.

THREE COMMON CAMPAIGN PROBLEMS—AND SUGGESTED SOLUTIONS

Problem I: Recruiting a General Campaign Chairperson

The Situation. Candidate No. 1 is a well-known, affluent public figure who has indicated his willingness to accept the position with the understanding that he would not be required to devote a great deal of time to the campaign. He would be willing, however, to preside at the kickoff and report meetings and would permit recruitment and solicitation letters to be written over his signature.

Candidate No. 2 is less known but has all of the personal attributes necessary and is willing and able to make the necessary commitment of time. Because she is less known, she lacks the broad contacts and prestige of Candidate No. 1.

Question. Which of these two should be chosen?

Answer. Possibly both. Candidate No. 1 should be requested to consider accepting the position of general campaign chairperson and Candidate No. 2 should be requested to consider the position of vice-chairperson. Together, they could form an effective top leadership team. Should Candidate No. 1 reject the position of chairperson, then Candidate No. 2 would be a far better selection for that position.

A prominent name on a letterhead will not do the job, and a "paper chairman" presiding at a meeting cannot be expected to create the atmosphere of excitement and urgency that is so important to the success of any campaign.

Problem II: Recruiting Corporate Leadership

The Situation. You are the general campaign chairperson, seeking an executive from a large corporation to head your corporation contributions division. A personal friend and fellow club member is a corporate vice president and has responded with enthusiasm to your request. Midway through the campaign, her corporate responsibilities suddenly are expanded, and she no longer has the time to devote to her campaign duties.

Question. What action should be taken?

Answer. There are three possible courses of action that should be considered and discussed at a special meeting, which should include the chairperson of the governing board's development committee and the staff campaign director, in addition to yourself (the general campaign chairperson):

1. Resignation of the corporate division chairperson and the subsequent promotion of one of her captains to the position.
2. Recruitment of a corporate captain to serve as division vice-chairman, so that the leadership team can be kept intact.
3. Suggestion that the corporate chairperson ask her superiors to consider lightening her business responsibilities temporarily until the conclusion of the campaign. The rationale for this suggestion would be the damaging effect on the company's image if the corporate campaign failed because of its chairperson's need to suddenly withdraw her leadership.

This situation could have been prevented if the request for the corporate chairperson's services was made initially to the company president, asking that he consider choosing your candidate or another executive. It should be made clear that the corporation's prestige and its resources will provide the necessary power base, rather than the individual who is appointed to the chair. In either case, the campaign becomes an official company project. The situation also could have been avoided if your candidate had sought the approval of her superiors prior to her acceptance.

Note: At any given time, a company president would be likely to prefer that certain company executives be given more (and certain executives be given less) public exposure through charitable voluntary service. In some cases, the president might be available, so it might be advisable to give him or her the first right of refusal.

Problem III: The Final Goal Has Not Been Met, but All Prospects Have Been Contacted

The Situation. Well before the official closing date of your campaign, reports indicate that all of your volunteer workers have completed their assignments. The total amount of contributions has fallen short of the goal, with more than a month remaining in the campaign period.

Question. What action should be taken?

Answer. A special committee meeting should be called by your general campaign chairperson to include the chairperson of the governing board's development council, chairpersons of the major campaign divisions, and the staff campaign director. The purpose of this meeting should be to plan a quick study to determine the following facts:

1. Has every volunteer made his or her contribution? How many have not? What is the total of last year's gifts from these volunteers?
2. Has every board member made a contribution?
3. Has your organization included all of its logical markets in the campaign? (Local merchants, corporations in the organization's service area, foundations whose stated interests match yours, individuals who have been helped by your programs?)
4. Have all of the prospects who were contacted been accounted for? How many are still outstanding? Was there any agreement or indication regarding the prospect's intentions at the time of contact? What is the total of their contributions last year?

The staff campaign director usually would be assigned to make the study and report the results to the committee at an action planning meeting to be held as soon as the facts are available. The elements of the plan would be governed by the results of the study.

The efforts of the volunteers already serving would be redirected to the following activities, forming special task forces when necessary.

1. To make their own contributions if they have not already done so (as requested by the general chairperson).
2. To request board members to make their contributions, if they have not already done so (as requested by the chairperson of the board's campaign council).
3. Appointment of a special task force to assemble prospects lists in new market areas and make necessary contacts.
4. Follow-ups by initial solicitors.

Note: If necessary, the campaign should be extended to allow for the completion of these remedial activities.

FINAL THOUGHTS

In closing this book, I would like to leave you with a final thought, with which most experienced development people are well familiar: The single objective of all is to produce situations where the right volunteers ask the right prospects to contribute money for the right causes. The volunteer is the key ingredient in development and has the potential power, truly, to "move mountains."

Here is just one case in point: One university was in the midst of completing its final planning for a major capital campaign to build a children's hospital. The goal was $7 million, of which $4 million was needed from the private sector, with government funding available for the $3 million balance. Brochures and other materials were printed, volunteer committees were formed, oriented, and ready to proceed with the advance gifts phase of the campaign. At this point, a trustee of the university reported that his contacts with members of two prominent families were successful. He had secured a commitment of $3 million from one family and $1 million from the other. With this striking achievement, the campaign was over.

Actually, as stated earlier, the entire concept of volunteerism is unique to the American way of life. It is a force that represents billions of dollars given and raised annually, and other valuable services, some of which money could never buy. Organizations everywhere, including yours, I'm sure, are constantly seeking the choice volunteer who is indeed our nation's most important product. When a volunteer appears at your organization's doorstep, be sure that you are prepared to convert his or her talents and energies to maximum productivity in the accomplishment of your mission.

APPENDIX A: SAMPLE MASTER CAMPAIGN PLAN

DEVELOPING A MASTER CAMPAIGN PLAN

Every campaign needs a plan. The outline of a plan that follows was designed for use by a large educational institution to combine the elements of the traditional single-phased fundraising campaign with a long-range multiphased development program. It is included as a model to assist you in structuring your own campaign plan, be it a long-range campaign for combined programmatic, capital and endowment needs, an annual fund campaign, or a capital campaign. The basic principles apply to all.

The body of this plan briefly touches on each of its components. Comprehensive chapters on most of the topics are contained elsewhere in this book.

SAMPLE OUTLINE FOR A MASTER CAMPAIGN PLAN

Table of Contents

Preface
Objectives
Goal Structure
Responsibility for the Campaign
Organizational Structure
Sources of Volunteers
Necessary Precampaign Activities

Recruitment of Volunteers

Orientation of Volunteers

Method of Solicitation

Solicitation Sequence

Public Relations

Acknowledgment of Contributions and Volunteer Services

Operational Timetable

PREFACE

The following plan has been designed to combine the elements of the traditional single-phased fund-raising campaign for our new basic sciences building with a multiphased development program, which will be ongoing.

Our basic objective is to develop a strong, well-coordinated base of support that will provide continuity in fund-raising for the operating needs of our institution, an intensive effort to meet our present capital needs, a continuous program to build our endowment, and subsequent special campaigns to meet our future needs, both capital and programmatic.

All of this will require careful planning and a great deal of hard work, but we feel that our institution has the capability to achieve our goals for a number of reasons, including the following:

- A long and distinguished record of pioneering and service as a university.
- The dimension of program innovation that few other institutions possess in the depth that we do.
- An able and dedicated board of trustees.
- A demonstrated need for the kind of health personnel education and training that we are providing now and new programs that are being planned.
- A strong and well-credentialed faculty.
- An enthusiastic alumni organization which has approximately 3,000 members and which already has made a strong commitment to the campaign.

- A wide network of teaching affiliations and working relationships with outstanding institutions and organizations.
- The endorsement and support of standard-setting organizations that we may use as references in our contacts with corporate foundations and other prospects.
- A growing base of support from the private sector, including 125 associates who contribute $1,000 or more annually.
- A loyal, 30-member woman's board with a 600-member auxiliary.

CAMPAIGN PLAN

I. Objectives

A. General

1. To form and establish a comprehensive and ongoing program of fund development that will enable our institution to meet its short- and long-range needs in the following areas:
   a. Operational (annual)
   b. Capital
   c. Endowment

B. Specific

1. The construction of our new $_____ basic sciences facility

II. Goal Structure

A. Dollar goal will be broken down and assigned to operating campaign divisions.

B. Whenever possible, goals should be determined for each major prospect by rating committees or by the solicitor to whom the prospect is assigned.

C. Approximately 85 percent of our goal should be obtained from 15 percent of our donors.

D. Recommended gift tables should be determined with the input of our campaign leadership to help maintain necessary levels of giving.

III. Responsibility for the Building Fund Campaign

A. The Board of Trustees of the University of course has basic responsibility for all fund development programs, as well as every other policy, program, and activity of the university.

1. Board Committee on Fund Development (This should be a standing committee of the board, responsible for recommending, and implementing, all fund-raising policies and programs for board approval.)

IV. Organizational Structure

A. General Campaign Chairperson

1. Alumni division

2. Corporations and foundations

3. Parents' division

4. Individual gifts, legacies, and bequests

5. Associates

6. Board of trustees

7. Woman's board

8. Faculty

9. Local community

10. Large cities or regional areas

V. Sources of Volunteers

A. Board of trustees

B. Alumni

C. Woman's board

D. Members of the faculty

E. Parents

    F. Associates

    G. Individuals who have indicated their interest in the University mission (past donors)

    H. New friends recruited by members of our institutional family and our campaign leadership

    I. Individuals who have been served by our university

VI. Sources of Support

    A. Past donors

    B. Board of trustees

    C. Woman's board

    D. Alumni, their families, and certain patients

    E. Faculty and administration

    F. Parents

    G. Corporations, including those with which we have contractual relationships

    H. Foundations whose stated purposes relate to our programs or objectives

    I. Others who are considered to be prospective donors by members of the university family

    J. Businesses, professions, clubs, organizations, and individuals in the community

    K. Bank trust officers

    L. Major law firms

    M. Certain accounting firms that advise clients on philanthropic matters

    N. Certain insurance companies that advise customers on various forms of deferred giving

Note: Initial questionnaire was sent to our institutional family by our board chairperson requesting their recommendations for additions to our prospect lists. This produced a total of 95 prospects recommended by a total of 22 who responded. A similar questionnaire will be mailed in the future, and our lists will be expanded further by recommendations from volunteers as they are enrolled and oriented into our campaign organization.

VII. Necessary Precampaign Activities

A. Appointment of board committee on fund development

B. Appointment of general campaign chairperson

C. Formation of campaign cabinet

D. Review amendment and approval of campaign plan by chairperson of the board, the general campaign chairperson, members of the board committee on fund development, and the board of trustees

E. Procurement of pacesetting advance gifts

F. Preparation of case statement, including identification of specific goals and needs, both fund-raising and programmatic

G. Determination of operational timetable, beginning with the formal announcement (appropriate kickoff event) and including the various stages of the campaign

H. Intensification of public relations program for purposes of ongoing cultivation

I. Expansion and refinement of prospect lists

J. Preparation of campaign materials

1. Prospectus (capital brochure)

2. Special alumni fund-raising device

3. Volunteer workers' handbook

4. Special visual displays, such as photographs, renderings, and models

5. Standard forms for recording and reporting gifts, volunteer recruitment, prospect assignments, and acknowledgment of both gifts and volunteer service rendered (includes standard and special pledge cards)

VIII. Recruitment of Volunteers

A. This would be accomplished in the traditional chain of command sequence, with a clear understanding by the person being recruited as to what his or her specific responsibilities will be.

B. During the course of the recruiting process, assistance from the department of development will be available upon request.

C. Detailed guidelines for recruiting will be included in all orientation sessions of campaign unit chairpersons at all levels of leadership.

IX. Orientation of Volunteers

A. Methods

1. Series of small meetings within each major campaign division

2. Individually, where necessary

B. Objectives

1. To inform

2. To motivate

C. Content of orientation sessions

1. Comprehensive information about our institution

2. Comprehensive information about the campaign

3. Explanation of specific assignments

4. Distribution of campaign materials and explanation of their use

X. Method of Solicitation

A. There is only one successful method of solicitation, and that is having the right individual make a personal call on the right prospect.

XI. Solicitation Sequence

A. Advance pacesetting contributions

1. This should be preceded by careful identification of major prospects and determination of amounts to be sought and who the most effective solicitor(s) would be in each case

B. Board of trustees, as planned by the chairperson

C. Alumni, as planned by a special alumni committee

D. Woman's board, as planned by its chairperson

E. Faculty, as planned by a special faculty committee

F. Parents, as planned by an appropriate parents' committee

G. Corporations and foundations

1. Within the regional area

2. Nationwide

H. Individual gifts

Note: Requests for legacies, bequests, and other forms of planned giving will be made in accordance with plans that will be constructed by a special committee as indicated in our organizational charts. This constitutes a vitally important element of our entire fund development program as evidenced by general estimates that the ten largest (most affluent) universities in the nation have received 80 percent of their endowment funds through legacies.

XII. Public Relations

A. In order to provide the visibility, image development, and back-up that our campaign will need, it is recommended that our public relations activities be intensified.

XIII. **Acknowledgment of Contributions of Money, Volunteer Efforts, and Special Assistance from Friends of the University—Including the Press**

A. All contributions will be promptly acknowledged in the following way:

1. By an official receipt

2. By a letter of appreciation from the chairperson of the board of trustees

3. By an additional letter from the person who secured the gift, especially when a substantial contribution has been made

B. All volunteers will receive appropriate expressions of appreciation in one or more of the following ways:

1. By letters of appreciation from the chairperson of the board of trustees and/or from the general campaign chairperson

2. By presentation of distinguished service awards or certificates of appreciation at special meetings

Note: Contributors and volunteers will be placed on our mailing lists, so that they can be kept informed about the state of our university. These individuals will represent a rich resource for future support and participation in future programs.

XIV. **Operational Timetable**

A. A realistic operational timetable cannot be constructed until after our general campaign chairperson has been appointed and can add his or her input as well as the input of the campaign cabinet to this crucially important element of our campaign.

Campaign Organizational Chart

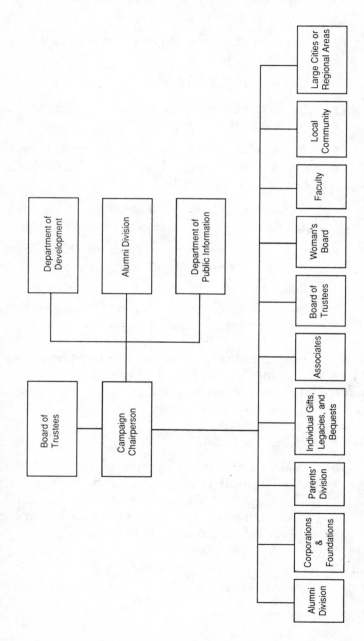

Campaign Cabinet

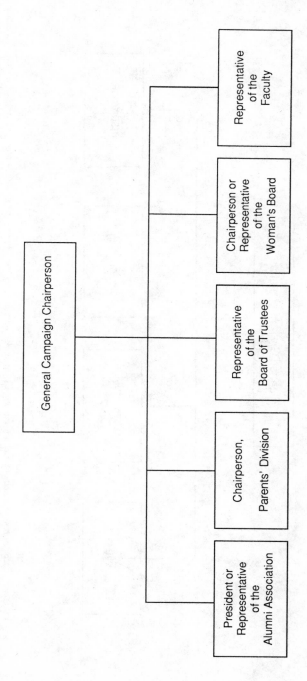

Suggested Organizational Chart for Subcommittee on Planned Giving

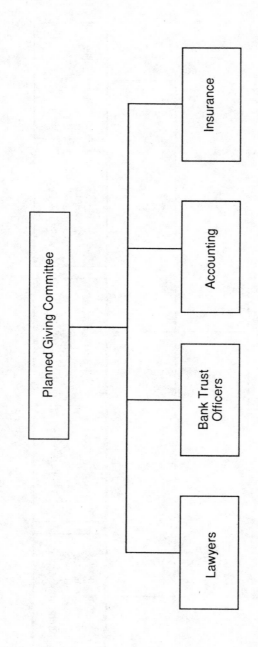

Note: A campaign subcommittee should be formed for the purpose of implementing informational programs directed to bank trust officers, attorneys, major accounting firms and certain insurance companies with a view toward the development of a legacy and bequest program including deferred giving of all forms. This subcommittee should include persons who are actively involved or who have broad knowledge of the fields indicated above.

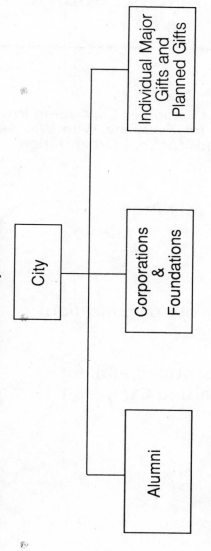

Suggested Campaign Organizational Chart for Certain Cities That Will Be Designated as Regional Bases of Operation

City

Alumni

Corporations & Foundations

Individual Major Gifts and Planned Gifts

Volunteer Resources:
- Associates
- Alumni
- Parents
- Trustees
- Other friends

Campaign Prospects:
- Associates
- Alumni
- Parents
- Certain Corporations and Foundations
- Other Friends
- New prospects (suggested by members of our institutional family)

APPENDIX B:
VOLUNTEER HANDBOOK FOR FUND-RAISING CAMPAIGN

Suggested Copy for a Pamphlet Containing Instructions and Guidance for Everyone Who Will Be Involved in Raising Funds for Your Organization

Cover Page

(Name of Your Organization)

Volunteer Handbook for Fund-Raising Campaign

MEMORANDUM

From: Chairman of the Board of Trustees or
      Campaign Chairman
To: Campaign Workers

We are deeply grateful for your cooperation and assistance in our fund-raising campaign.

The key to the success of any campaign—and indeed our richest resource—is the enthusiastic, well-informed volunteer—you!

Important also is the need for all of us to follow some basic guidelines that will help us to make maximum use of our resources within a uniform and orderly campaign structure.

Accordingly, we hope you will read this pamphlet carefully and consider its contents before contacting your prospects.

1. **Planning Your Approach**
   - Remember that each solicitation comprises a capsule campaign within itself and should be planned and executed accordingly.
   - In presenting our organization's story, try to stress those areas in which your prospect appears to have a special interest. A thorough review and study of our literature and other information obtained through your orientation will help you to do this.
   - In planning your approach, decide whether you wish to see the prospect alone or whether you wish to have others accompany you. If you do wish resource people to accompany you on the first visit, make arrangements through our Department of Development for assistance from an appropriate member of our campaign organization or our organizational family.

2. **Suggested Procedure for Solicitation**
   - Make your own thoughtful gift first.
   - Make each call a personal one. People give to people, and regardless of how well you know the prospect, the best results are secured only through a face-to-face discussion.

- Make an appointment to meet with your prospect in whatever setting you feel will be most appropriate, over lunch or dinner, or in the office or home. Where you feel this would be helpful, combine the meeting with a visit to our organization so that the prospect can see our programs in action. An informal tour can be arranged through our Department of Development.
- In some instances, after the initial meeting it may be wise to leave printed material and ask for an opportunity to continue the discussion after the material has been studied, and/or after a site visit.
- Decide whether you wish to involve resource people in this second meeting, especially if you seek a large contribution.
- Respond to all questions, but do not attempt to answer questions for which you do not have the necessary information. Rather, indicate that they will be answered fully either by you or by someone else at a subsequent time.

3. **The Presentation and Documentation of Our Case to the Prospect**
   - Our campaign brochure and supporting materials contain all of the basic information about our organization that should be necessary for most potential donors.
   - In discussing our current and projected needs with your prospect, be sure to identify all of the different ways in which financial support can be given. These are summarized here (not in order of priority):
   - A. Unrestricted contributions of cash, securities, or property.
   - B. Earmarked contributions of cash or securities for: (substitute your own needs for the ones that follow)
     - A building or one of its components, e.g., an entire floor, library or sections thereof (including books and periodicals), auditorium, classrooms, conference rooms
     - General endowment
     - Department chairs or other academic endowments

- Scholarships
- Lectureships
- Student loan funds
- Other programs or facilities that need support

C. Legacies, bequests, and/or various other planned gifts, both unrestricted and restricted (earmarked)

Note: All inquiries, suggestions, or expressions of interest in these or other named grant opportunities should be directed to our chief executive officer or development officer through campaign channels.

- Where feasible, request a specific amount based on what you feel the prospect's potential might be. In doing this, it might be helpful to refer to pacesetting contributions that already have been secured, a list of which can be obtained from our Department of Development.
- If it appears indicated, suggest a subsequent meeting that would include another resource person who could help to strengthen certain points in your presentation in which your prospect has evidenced a particular interest—especially in cases where there is interest in having a facility, unit, or program within our organization named in memory of, or in honor of, a loved one, or in the donor's own name. This meeting can be arranged through our Department of Development.

4. **Negotiating the Contribution or Pledge**
   - Checks should be made payable to our organization.
   - Contributions may be paid over an extended period of time (3 years, 5 years, etc.).
   - Arrangements for all contributions of securities or property, legacies, bequests, and other forms of planned gifts should be made with appropriate officials through our Department of Development.
   - All contributions should be directed to:

     [insert name of campaign chairperson]
     [address]

- All contributions will be acknowledged by [insert name of chairperson]. In addition, you may wish to make your own personal acknowledgment to those individuals whose gifts were made as a result of your efforts. If you have any questions or need more information, please write or call:

[insert name and address]

Note: In order to avoid duplication of effort and general confusion, solicit only those prospects who have been assigned to you or selected by you and cleared with our Department of Development.

If you need assistance, advice, or any additional information regarding any aspect of the campaign, please contact your unit chairperson or:

_____ name and title
_____ address
_____ telephone (business)
_____ telephone (home)

OR

Name, title, address, and telephone numbers of staff, campaign director, or the individual serving in that capacity

Again, your efforts are deeply appreciated and will be instrumental in helping us to [describe your program objective].

_____
Name and signature of chairperson of governing board and/or campaign chairperson

INDEX